Putting the Pieces Together Again

Teens Write About Surviving Rape

By Youth Communication

Edited by Hope Vanderberg

Putting the Pieces Together Again

Executive Editors
Keith Hefner and Laura Longhine

Contributing Editors
Nora McCarthy, Rachel Blustain, Philip Kay,
Andrea Estrepa, and Kendra Hurley

Layout & Design
Efrain Reyes, Jr. and Jeff Faerber

Cover Art
Paulina Korkuz

For reprint information, please contact Youth Communication.

ISBN 978-1-933939-86-5

Second, Expanded Edition
The first edition of this book was entitled "It Also Happened to Me."

Printed in the United States of America

Youth Communication®
New York, New York
www.youthcomm.org

Table of Contents

Introduction

"I know there are other girls who have been raped and are too ashamed to tell anyone," writes the teen author of "Telling Someone Helped Me Feel Better," the second story in this book. "But I'll tell you this: When you speak to someone, it's a relief."

Girls aged 16-19 are four times more likely than the general population to be victims of rape or attempted rape, according to the Rape Abuse and Incest National Network. And nearly half of rape victims in the U.S. are under 18. Most of them know their attackers.

But while rape is tragically common among teens, many survivors feel completely alone. In this book, teen rape survivors write about their feelings of guilt, shame, fear, and isolation, as well as how they began to find support and heal.

According to psychologist Patti Feuereisen, who was interviewed by teen writer Mimi Callaghan, victims of date rape often blame themselves, while stranger rape can cause victims to be in a state of panic in everyday life. Some victims go into denial, pretending nothing happened. Male victims have a particularly difficult time admitting what happened, because many believe only girls can be raped.

Many survivors stay silent because they feel they are the only ones who have experienced this, because they are ashamed, because they feel the rape was somehow their fault. And their silence isolates them even more.

But while the scar of what happened will always be there, Feuereisen says, you can heal. The first step is talking to someone, whether it's a counselor, a best friend, or a parent, so that you can begin to work through your feelings.

For all the writers in this book, speaking out—either verbally or through writing their story—was crucial to their healing process.

The anonymous author of "Dream Guy, Nightmare

Experience" is only 13 when she's raped by a boyfriend she's had for five days. She finally finds some relief from her pain when she talks to some friends and adults about it. In "Why Are You Doing This, Mr. Jones?" the author is raped repeatedly by her social worker in the foster care system, who keeps her in a constant state of fear by telling her the agency will never believe her word over his. It takes her six months to break her silence, but when she does tell a counselor, she learns that Mr. Jones was wrong—people do believe her.

In "Haunted," the male writer recalls being raped by his babysitter's son at age 8. He tries to block it out for years, but it resurfaces again and again until he finally has the courage to confront the memory. "It's messed up that someone can come into your life for so brief a time and screw everything up so much," he writes. "I can't get back what was stolen. But I'm writing this story because I also know that if I keep it hidden from myself, the abuse will only surface in more painful ways."

The stories in this book convey not only the horror of rape, but the strength of the survivors who wrote about it so that they could finally move on. We hope their stories give other survivors of rape the courage to confront their own experiences and begin healing.

In some stories, names and some identifying details have been changed.

AaronLily

Dream Guy, Nightmare Experience

By Anonymous

I'm lying on the floor in a dark room, unable to move. Then I see him standing over me, laughing. I try to move but I'm paralyzed. He gets closer and closer and right when he's about to kiss me, I wake up screaming. After that I'm too upset to go back to sleep, so I sit up and cry all night.

My nightmares aren't as vivid as before, but they're there. Just when I think it's finally over, the memories come back to haunt me. I keep thinking that maybe I could have done something to prevent it. Maybe if I hadn't been such a sucker for a happy ending. Maybe if I had thought ahead. Maybe...Maybe...

He lived in the neighborhood and was always hanging around. I used to see him in the morning, before school. He was about 16, kind of tall, with short, dark hair, and the most beautiful gray eyes I'd ever seen. He'd say "hi" when he saw me and even though I didn't really know him, I started to like him. Occasionally I'd stop and talk to him—nothing too personal. We talked about the movies we'd seen, music, and stuff like that. I began to look forward to our little talks and was disappointed when I didn't see him around the school. I was 13 at the time.

I'll never forget the look Eric gave me afterward, like he was proud of what he had done.

One day, he was waiting for me outside after school. I was talking to my friend Charlene and I pretended that I didn't see him, even though he kept trying to get my attention. I don't know why—maybe I didn't want Charlene to know I had a crush on him.

After I said goodbye to Charlene, I walked slowly to the end of the block. "Hello," he called out to me.

I turned slowly and smiled at him. "Hi, Eric," I said shyly.

"Where are you going?" he asked.

I told him I was going to the subway station. He asked if he could walk me there, and, being the lovesick puppy that I was, I said, "Sure."

Eric carried my books and we talked all the way to the subway station. When we arrived, he asked if he could have my phone number. I was so excited that I gave it to him without any hesitation.

He called that night. We talked for at least two hours. Eric told me that he lived with his aunt and his brother. He said he'd been wanting to talk to me for a while, that he liked me and wanted to get together sometime. That phone call made me the happiest person in the world. After I got off the phone with him, I called some of my friends and told them. Being liked by a guy made me feel important.

The next time I saw him, he walked me to the subway station

again and we talked some more. Then he kissed me goodbye. It was just a small kiss, but it made me feel wonderful. I was convinced he was a great guy.

Eric called me again that night. We talked for a while and, just as I hoped, he "popped the question."

"Yes! I'll go out with you!" I half screamed. For the rest of the night I was so happy, I was practically floating in mid-air. "Somebody loves me," I thought.

We were "boyfriend and girlfriend" for a grand total of five days. He called me and we saw each other throughout the week. Then after school on Friday, he was waiting for me in our usual meeting place, on the corner by the schoolyard. He said he wanted to take me someplace special that afternoon. I was thrilled. I thought maybe we would go to the movies or something. "But first," he said, "we have to stop by my house for a minute."

It was a pretty big apartment, but it looked like it hadn't been cleaned in years. He brought me into the kitchen and got a glass of water. Then we went into the living room and sat on a sofa with the stuffing coming out of it. He told me to leave my books on the floor. Then he turned on the TV and shut off all the lights and said, "We'll go in a minute. I'm tired. I want to rest for a second. Sit down with me." So, I did.

We sat in the darkness and watched TV for a while. I asked him where his aunt and his brother were. He stared at me with those eyes and replied, "Out," plain and simple. He was acting kind of weird, but I didn't want to say anything because I thought he might get mad or something. He took my hand and started to kiss me. At first it was kind of nice. But then he started getting too aggressive, putting his hands in places they didn't belong.

I remember thinking to myself, "This doesn't feel right. What's he doing?" I started getting scared and told Eric to stop. But he didn't. I tried pushing him away, but he was a lot bigger than me. He forced himself on top of me and pulled my pants down. No matter how much I struggled, he wouldn't let up.

He held me down by the shoulders and raped me. I was crying and screaming, "No! Stop! Please stop!" But he wouldn't. Exhausted from crying and trying to get him off me, I stared into the blackness, tears sliding off of my cheeks.

It happened almost three years ago, but I still think about it as though it were yesterday. I have to stop asking myself if it was my fault.

It all happened very fast. As soon as I could, I fixed my pants, tried to wipe the tears away, and got the hell out of there. I walked the eight blocks to the subway station and waited for the subway in a daze. I kept telling myself that it didn't really happen, that it couldn't really happen—not to me.

On the subway, a guy pressed up against me and tried to talk to me. I just turned around and walked through to the next car. Then I caught some girl looking at me, like she knew. I gave her a really ugly stare and she looked away, embarrassed.

When I finally made it home, the first thing I did was jump in the shower. I washed my entire body, but I just couldn't seem to feel clean. I dried myself off and put on some clean clothes. Then I looked at the clothes I was wearing at the time it happened. I noticed blood on my pants and shirt. I had a small cut on my chest and my legs were scraped up—I guess from struggling. I took the clothes, balled them up, and put them in a plastic bag. I carried them to the incinerator and threw them out. Then I went into my room, lay down on my bed, and cried. Thank God my mother wasn't home.

I didn't want to think about it, but I couldn't help it. I'll never forget the look Eric gave me afterward, like he was proud of what he had done. Then something else popped into my mind: what if I get pregnant? I closed my eyes and tried to block the thought. (Thankfully, I wasn't pregnant, but I was really scared for a while.)

I saw him once more when I went to the store with Charlene one day after school. I was getting some juice and, while I was walking up to the counter to pay for it, he and two of his friends came into the store. My heart raced and I dropped the bottle. It smashed on the floor, but I didn't hear it. Charlene grabbed me and pulled me out of there. She knew something was wrong, but she kept her mouth shut. I didn't leave my house for a few weeks after that. I was afraid I might see him again. Playing sick seemed to be the only escape.

One day my best friend was over at my house and I decided to tell her. I just couldn't keep this horrible secret inside of me any longer. "Kate, I need to tell you something," I said. I took a deep breath and sat down. I tried to go slowly, but the words raced out of my mouth. "I was going out with this guy and I thought he was really nice but he wasn't. Kate, you're my best friend and I want you to help me. I was raped."

Kate just stared at me in shock. Then the expression on her face changed to one of disbelief. "Well," she said, "how do you know if he really raped you?" I couldn't believe it. My best friend doubting me, almost accusing me of lying. Things between us were never the same from then on. I can't say that I hate her, because I don't. I just don't talk to her—about anything.

Eventually I told some other friends and a few adults. I'm happy to say that all of them really helped me. They always listened when I needed to talk, anytime. Even if it was 3:30 in the morning, and I had trouble sleeping, I could call them up and they'd help me get through it. Now I regret not speaking to anyone sooner.

It happened almost three years ago, but I still think about it as though it were yesterday. I have to stop asking myself if it was my fault, if I "asked for it." It wasn't my fault. I didn't ask for it. I had no control over the situation. The only thing I did wrong was wait so long to get help.

Rape is a horrible thing. It can happen to anyone. And yes, you can be raped by someone you know. One minute you're watching TV, riding along in a car, getting help with homework. The next minute you're fighting to get away, gasping for breath, staring off into the blackness. If it does happen to you, remember, it's not your fault. Tell someone fast. Get help. It'll really make a difference later on.

The writer was in high school when she wrote this story.

Telling Someone Helped Me Feel Better

By Anonymous

When I was a freshman, I was raped in my school. I was going to the bathroom and then, the next thing I knew, I was found in the basement with my tights ripped and my pants down.

All I can remember is some guy whispering in my ear that that is what a girl gets when she tries to play a guy. I believe the guy must have hit me and I passed out. Otherwise, knowing me, I would have put up a real good fight.

A janitor found me in the boiler room, where the janitors' lockers were. It was a place that was popular with students who wanted to have sex in the school, and I guess he thought I was a fast girl who did that kind of thing.

When he found me, he kept asking me why I was down there, and told me to stop cutting class before he called security. When

I saw where I was, I was shocked. I ran to the bathroom to get myself together, and it began to kick in what had happened. I cried to let out the tears of anger. I felt so ashamed.

Thinking it was my fault, I didn't tell anyone about it. At first, I didn't even want to be around anyone because I felt like they would be able to see that I was dirty and not worth being around. I didn't go to school for two weeks. I told my mother I was sick, and she didn't make a big deal about it.

At school, no one knew what happened, but I felt like everyone knew and was staring at me, and that made me feel even dirtier inside.

The idea of the rape got to me more than the actual act of being raped. I know that might sound strange, but it's the truth. The thought of someone taking my power and strength made me feel worthless. I felt dirty from the act, but the feeling of being powerless hurt me the most.

I grew up with a lot of guys who were always picking on me, and I was always trying to be a woman with a man's strength and attitude, showing that I had no fear. People in my school knew me as the girl who didn't take anything from any human being.

I thought I was too tough for anyone to think of violating me. Not being able to defend myself made me feel really weak and vulnerable.

All I could think about was, "How was I carrying myself—was I acting like a cheap girl who wouldn't mind a guy doing that to me? Did I bring it on myself?" That was running through my mind constantly.

And I was angry all the time. As soon as I got home after the rape, all the anger started to build up inside me.

At first my hatred was with everyone, but later it was just with men. I hated everything about them. They were my enemies and I wanted to destroy any man who came my way.

At times I would snap on guys for no reason at all. Once a guy was looking at my breasts and I punched him in the face. I felt he was really disrespecting me, and I was afraid he was getting dirty thoughts about me and might try something. I would just curse out guys who tried to talk to me.

I would talk about men like they were dogs and talk about killing any guy I didn't like for some little reason. I felt like I could never show love to any man, and for a while, I didn't want to show love to anyone.

I didn't trust anyone who tried to be close to me. I felt like they were invading my space and that made me want to explode. I thought everyone was trying to find me out, and that was my biggest fear. So I pushed everyone away.

When my friends and family asked me what was wrong, I would say, "Why are you so damn nosy? Leave me alone." They were wondering what the hell was wrong with me, but I wouldn't let them find out.

All I could think was, "How was I carrying myself—was I acting like a cheap girl who wouldn't mind a guy doing that to me?"

I also felt that I couldn't even love myself, and that I couldn't live anymore. I wanted to commit suicide almost every day. I feel like that is a stage you go through when something so terrible happens to you. You feel like you've lost all your self-respect and dignity. I didn't want to face another day feeling like I wasn't anything.

I was so scared and alone, having all those thoughts running through my mind, and not knowing what to think or how to feel about myself. The feelings of being dirty, worthless and defenseless tore me down emotionally.

I thought I was never going to get over it. I felt like the anger building up in me was allowing the devil to take me over. The negativity I was showing to everyone around me wasn't making me feel happy; instead, I felt worse knowing that I kept feeling so down and the old sweet, positive side couldn't seem to come out anymore.

After a few months, I gradually realized that if I showed that I was down, people would keep wanting to know what was wrong with me. So I tried to act like everything was all right with me. But inside, I was a miserable human being who felt that she was the one to blame for what had happened.

I knew I didn't want to let the negativity take me over. I wanted the hatred that I had for myself and for others to leave me. I tried everything I could think of to make that happen.

I would tell myself that nothing ever happened. I would take things apart and put them back together, like my VCR and Walkman, and my nephew's boat model and classic car models. I would draw clothing designs to keep my mind occupied. When I concentrated on things like that, it kept my mind off my emotions.

I also used to write notes to myself to express my feelings, because I couldn't talk about what happened.

About nine months later, even though I really didn't trust anyone, I began dating a male friend of mine who I'd known for years. I thought it would help me stop feeling so afraid of all men. Dating him did help, in a way. I felt I could trust getting close to him because he didn't get into my business.

He felt females had issues that no one could help them with, so when I would act mean or down, he didn't try to find out what was wrong. He'd just leave me alone. It made me feel safe to be close to him while keeping my secret.

Eventually, I started praying to God for help. My mother would always say, "If you have a problem with anything, go to God and ask for help." I took my mother's words of advice. I felt like I was putting myself in someone else's hands. This made me feel hopeful that I could get better.

Hope made me feel as if I was healing every day. Even though I had my bad days, I would just stay to myself until that feeling would leave.

Praying allowed me to go through my bad moments of anger and think about the good moments, too. The more I prayed, the more positively I felt, and the more it seemed that good times came around for me. Slowly, my attitude started to change.

The change was damn sure not easy. For me to try to tell you all that I had to do to get over this, it brings so many feelings back into my heart that I tried hard to remove.

Finally, I realized that trying to fix everything on my own wasn't going to work. I decided it was time to take the burden off my shoulders. It took me three years to open my mouth and speak about being raped. When I decided to open up, I was so afraid.

I was afraid if I told people, they'd blame me. I also thought they'd be mad that I hadn't told them when it happened. I still felt ashamed, too, but I had started to understand that bad things can happen to you, even if you don't deserve it, and that sometimes you can't do a damn thing about it.

I decided to tell my mom first. I didn't like the idea that she didn't know what had happened to her own daughter.

I couldn't just come out and tell her, so I wrote her a letter. She always said, "If you can't talk about something, then write it down." So I wrote what happened and apologized for taking so long to tell her.

When I gave her the note, I was getting into the shower, because I didn't want to look her in her eyes while she read it. When I came out, she was sitting on the sofa in tears. She said, "I would have done something about it!"

She didn't ask many questions, because she knew it might be hard for me to talk about it and she didn't want me to get flashbacks. And I was glad, because I didn't want to talk about the details. It was not a brush off, but a step toward moving on.

After that, my mom and I got friendlier. She said, "I don't care what it is, you can come to me. I'm going to talk to you as a woman." Now we talk about everything. Sometimes I'm like, "I don't want to talk about this—you're my mother!" But I feel much more comfortable and I don't have to hide.

It's a relief, too, because my mother is 62, and she has so much wisdom. I didn't want to listen to her for a long time, but she helps me out a lot. Now she'll give me advice and then say, "You shouldn't do this, but I know you teenagers will do it anyway." And I have to prove to her that I can listen.

When I opened up to her, my mother was like a true friend. She gave me a sense of joy and happiness I had been missing.

For a long time, my friends had realized that something was seriously wrong with me, so a little while after I told my mom, they got together and kept asking me until I began talking. I wouldn't have told them, but once I started talking, I just let all my feelings go.

While I was telling them what had happened, I began to feel very nasty. My whole body began to shake, and it felt like people were touching me. I started crying and I couldn't stop. I also got flashbacks of hearing the whisper in my ear.

One of my friends said, "You need a lot of love," and she was right.

My friends kept telling me to let all my tears out so I could at least feel free of one burden—the burden of holding my emotions in.

When I'd told the whole story, they said things that made me feel better, like, "It's not your fault, there's a lot of sick men out there," and, "Whenever you have problems, tell us." For a while, they called me every day and spent a lot of time with me. If I went somewhere, I didn't go by myself. They had my back.

One of my friends said, "You need a lot of love," and she was right.

My friends' reactions were so good. They were like big sisters. I found out I could trust them and count on them. I had never really trusted females. A lot of girls talk too much and backstab each other, so with all females I had a border that I wouldn't let them cross. But I'm glad I finally did.

The love and care they showed would have made anyone feel worth a million dollars. They helped me to get over it by talking to me, letting me know it wasn't my fault, and being there when I needed someone to lean on.

That helped me feel more secure and strong, show the sweet side of my character, and give other people the chance to become my friend.

I wish I had been able to tell my family and friends earlier. If I had told someone right away, I could have gotten help. I wouldn't have felt like no one could understand what I was going through, and I wouldn't have felt so alone.

If I had told, I don't think I would have been hating men for so long. And I wouldn't have been hating myself. Plus, maybe they would have caught the guy.

I know there are other girls who have been raped and are too ashamed to tell anyone. They don't know how others might look at them if they tell. But I'll tell you this: When you speak to someone, it's a relief.

Being raped can affect you for a long time afterward. You need to get support. Talking about it to someone you trust will help you get on with your life.

The author was 17 when she wrote this story.

Why Are You Doing This, Mr. Jones?

By Anonymous

After having my baby at the age of 17, I had no place to go. I had no choice but to go into a mother-infant program. (It's a group home where young mothers live with their children.)

When I entered the mother-infant home with my child, I was scared and nervous. I had never been in foster care before. But the first week went pretty good. A staff member named Ms. Days helped me take care of my newborn baby, while Mr. Jones, my social worker, helped me try to figure out what I wanted to do with my life. He made me feel right at home, and in my heart I felt that I could trust him.

I knew right then and there that I hadn't made a mistake by having a baby, because with the help of the staff I could continue with my schoolwork as I raised my child.

But there were times that I would look at my daughter and tell myself how much she looked like my mother. After I put my daughter to sleep, I found myself thinking about the fun things me and my mother used to do together.

I missed my mother so much that I was crying at night and very depressed. I had to find a way to see her, because a year and two months without contact was a long time, and she didn't even know that I had a baby. I never understood why she threw me out of the house.

I told Mr. Jones about crying at night and that I needed to see my mother. He asked me for my mother's address and phone number. Then he told me not to worry, because he was going to try his best to get in touch with my mother. I was pleased.

Then two days passed, the worst two days of my life. I didn't hear from Mr. Jones. I wondered if he got in contact with my mother, and how she would react when he told her that I had a baby. And then I had to deal with the baby crying. I was going through hell.

After the third day, I finally received a phone call at night from my social worker, telling me that he called my mother. She was not home, Mr. Jones said, but he left a message.

I was mad that it took him three days to give me that message. I told him thanks for calling and was about to hang up, when Mr. Jones asked me if I was going to be at my house tomorrow. I told him, "Yeah, why?"

He said, "Because I'm supposed to check out the house and make sure that everything is OK, and I really want you to be there."

Around 12 p.m. the next day Mr. Jones and Ms. Days came to the house. We talked for a while, then all of a sudden it was quiet. As I went into the kitchen to get something to drink, I felt Mr. Jones staring at me hard. I tried to pay it no mind.

Mr. Jones didn't leave the house until after 1 p.m. I was glad when he left. I went downstairs to check the mailbox, because I was expecting a letter from my baby's father, who was in jail at the time.

I received three letters that day. Two were from my baby's father, and the other one was from someone who wrote on the outside, "Open it up and look what's inside."

I thought the letter was from my baby's father, too, but I was wrong. It was from Mr. Jones. He'd written that he found me attractive. Now I knew there was something wrong.

Later that night I received a phone call from Mr. Jones. He told me that he had gotten in touch with my mother, and that she was kind of upset that I had had a baby and that she needed time to think about seeing me.

I was so happy to hear that Mr. Jones got in touch with her, but I was also afraid to ask him why he had written me the letter. I told him thanks and hung up the phone. I thought hanging up would give Mr. Jones a message, but it didn't.

One day soon after that, Mr Jones called and told me that my mother wanted me to come see her. He asked me if I felt comfortable if he came and picked me up. Like an a-hole, I told him yes. He told me to meet him at the subway station.

When he finally came and picked me up I was mad because he'd kept me waiting for about an hour. But in a way I didn't care because I was on my way to see my mother and she was going to see her first grandchild.

After driving across the Queensboro bridge, I could feel and see Mr. Jones looking at me hard, real hard, but for some reason I wasn't scared.

After coming off the bridge we were in the Bronx, instead of Manhattan where my mother lived. I asked Mr. Jones why we were in the Bronx. His reply was, "Because I live in the Bronx and I need to change my clothes before I go into Manhattan," he said.

He stopped in front of a blue building and told me that he didn't think that I should wait in the car for him because the neighborhood was really bad. So I agreed to go upstairs with him.

I went into his living room while he went into his bedroom. He asked me if I wanted anything to drink. I told him no, and then he started to talk about the carpet in his bedroom. He suggested I come and see it, so I laid my baby down on the couch, and went into his bedroom to see what he was talking about.

All of a sudden Mr. Jones started hugging me and telling me that I felt and smelled good. I told him to get off me and tried to force him away from me, but he wouldn't let me go.

I was screaming and yelling, thinking that somebody would hear me and come knocking on the door to see what was wrong, but nobody came. My baby didn't even wake up from my yells.

Mr. Jones forced me down on the bed and told me to shut up. He told me that he wanted some from me. I told him no, and asked him why was he doing this to me.

"You're supposed to be my social worker, you're supposed to help me, not try to have sex with me!"

His reply was, "It's after work hours and I'm not nobody's social worker now."

Then I said, "If you don't get off of me, I'm going to tell the people at the agency."

Mr. Jones had my hands gripped tight to the bed. He started kissing my neck and said, "Those people at the agency don't care about you. I'm your social worker and they ain't going to believe you."

I was really mad now. I really wanted this man off me, so I started kicking and tossing around. But it didn't work.

Mr. Jones continued to tell me about how the people at the agency don't care about me and my baby. I didn't believe him, until he started talking about one of the staff members in the house who used to hit on a girl and scream at her.

When the girl told the agency, Mr. Jones said that they believed the staff over the girl. He also told me that everything has to go through him, he's the one who has to call my mother to see if it's OK for me to come home on weekends.

"So who's going to believe," Mr. Jones said, "that I had sex with you?"

I started to think, "Why is the agency like this? Why do they treat us wrong?"

I also was thinking if I was to have sex with Mr. Jones, he would let me go on my weekend pass anytime, and I could come back to the house anytime I wanted, and Mr. Jones wouldn't say anything to me because we had done something together.

While I was still thinking about what to do, Mr. Jones started kissing my breast, then the kissing started to get heavier, and then he started to play with my legs. I wanted to scream, but I also wanted to go on a weekend pass with my mother. I was confused and didn't know what to do.

When Mr. Jones asked me if he could have some, I told him yes. I figured one time wouldn't hurt. I would just pretend that I wasn't there.

After he was finished, I was ready to go home. I felt sick and dirty.

When Mr. Jones dropped me off by the subway station in Queens, he told me that he would see me the next day and that I would definitely get to see my mother. I told him yeah, whatever, and walked away. I thought that night would be the first and last time that I would have sex with Mr. Jones, but I was wrong.

We continued to have intercourse for about two months. During those two months, Mr. Jones had me thinking that the agency didn't care about me and that he was the only one that I could trust, and I kept believing this for a while.

But one day Mr. Jones and I had unprotected intercourse and he came inside me. A couple of days later, I asked Mr. Jones, "Suppose I am pregnant? What should I do?"

His reply was, "Well, if you are pregnant, it ain't from me because I know I'm not the only one that's having sex with you."

That's when I finally realized that Mr. Jones was using me and abusing me.

He was my social worker. I had to ask him if I could stay

outside late or if I could leave my baby with my aunt, and whenever I asked him, Mr. Jones would say he would think about it. I knew what that meant. It meant that I had to have sex with him in order to get permission.

The final straw was when he told me that he would help me and my mother unite again together, but he never did. I was the one who called my mother to see how she was doing. The only thing Mr. Jones did was call her and tell her that I had a baby and that I was with his agency.

Mr. Jones started kissing my neck and said, "Those people at the agency don't care about you. I'm your social worker and they ain't going to believe you."

When I finally saw my mother, I asked Mr. Jones if I could spend the night at her house. Mr. Jones said he'd think about it, and for me to meet him downstairs so he could talk to me, but I knew what that really meant. I told him OK, but I never went to meet him.

That following Monday, Mr. Jones was upset with me and put me on restriction for two weeks. He said the only way that you can go outside is if you come to my house. I was mad because I knew he put me on restriction for that one time I didn't meet him downstairs. So I finally stopped having sex with him and had to deal with restriction for a while.

I didn't tell anybody that I had sex with Mr. Jones because, like he said, "Who would believe me over him?" But six months after the abuse began I was ripping up inside, both mentally and physically. I couldn't help but share my experience with somebody, so I told my counselor at high school what happened to me. I knew that I was in the wrong for letting Mr. Jones have sex with me, but I needed to tell somebody how I was feeling.

I thought my counselor would put me down and tell me how much I was in the wrong. Instead, she told me, "It's not your fault. He's supposed to help you. You were raped, because he made you do something that you didn't want to do. And not only were you raped, but you were abused mentally."

I felt good because I finally had somebody on my side. Mr. Jones had told me that nobody would ever believe me, but I guess he was wrong for the first time.

My counselor told me that she strongly felt that I should tell the people at my agency. "Mr. Jones should not get away with this," she said, "because if he did it to you, he could do it to someone else, and it might be even worse."

I didn't want everybody to know my business, but in a way I knew he did rape and abuse me, and that's something that I couldn't forget. So I agreed that I would tell on him. I wanted Mr. Jones to be put in jail. I agreed to tell my story, but only if my counselor was going to stick with me, and she agreed.

On the day of my appointment I couldn't help but cry. I told Sam, the head social worker at my agency, everything that was going on between me and Mr. Jones. I told Sam that I felt ashamed and embarrassed. Sam told me that I had no reason to feel that way. "If anybody should be ashamed and embarrassed," he said, "it's Mr. Jones." He told me not to worry because he would report it to children's services.

Two weeks after reporting Mr. Jones, I had an appointment to meet with a lawyer in Manhattan. My counselor came with me to make sure that everything went all right.

As soon as we arrived at the courthouse in Manhattan I was happy, because I knew that the lawyer would be on my side and that he or she would help me put Mr. Jones away. So I didn't have any fear in my heart.

But after I told the lawyer my story, she said, "I can imagine what you are going through and I want to help you the best way that I can. But your story isn't a case that can be handled, because you gave it up to him without him even having to take it from you. When somebody takes something from you and you say, 'No,' and they take it anyway, then that's what you call rape. But in your case, you were just used."

I told the lawyer that Mr. Jones had forced me down on his bed to have sex, but she said there was nothing she could do.

I was mad and upset and told the lawyer that Mr. Jones was right when he said, "Ain't nobody going to listen to you." Then I started to cry and kept asking myself, "Why did it have to be me?" My counselor couldn't help, but she rubbed my back and thanked the lawyer for trying to help me.

My counselor walked me downstairs and asked me if I would be all right. I told her yeah, knowing damn well this was eating me up alive, knowing that man was out free and didn't give a damn how he hurt and abused a girl 27 years younger than himself.

My counselor told me that we still had to go to children's services. They were the ones who could really determine whether or not Mr. Jones should be punished. I was so upset that I didn't even respond.

I thought my counselor would put me down and tell me how much I was in the wrong. Instead, she told me, "It's not your fault."

Three weeks later, I had another appointment with children's services. While they were asking me questions I felt relaxed, because every time I would stop or pause they would say, "It's OK, I can understand what you might be going through. Take your time; it's all right."

And after I finished my story one of them said, "No matter what, you should not feel ashamed of yourself, because what he did to you was wrong, and as soon as we go back to the office we are going to get started on this case."

I was glad but also sad, because Mr. Jones had been recently fired from the agency not because of what he did to me, but for other reasons. Still, I was beginning to feel more relaxed because I finally had the law on my side.

After two months, children's services asked to see me again. I was hoping to hear good news, but all they did was ask me if I could tell my story over again and to describe what Mr. Jones' house looked like.

They told me that when they interviewed Mr. Jones, he denied everything and told them that I was lying. They asked me to describe the house because that could be something they could use against him. They also told me that they would get in touch with me to tell me what happened.

It's been 19 months since then, and I haven't heard anything yet. I think they probably dropped the case, or else I would have heard something by now. Maybe they didn't have enough evidence or maybe they didn't know who to believe.

They probably have forgotten all about me, like Mr. Jones said they would. He was right—they don't even care about me and my baby, and I guess that's why he's still a loose man. He can find a job anywhere and just forget about the job he was fired from.

But as a teenager and as a mother I can't forget, because my past will always be by my side, no matter how hard I try to forget about it.

It's always going to be a part of me, and, as I watch my daughter grow up, I'm very confused. She's getting more beautiful each day, and as a mother I can't help but think about how it's going to be for her when she gets older.

I know she's going to have lots of boyfriends, and one day she might have a male friend who she trusts, and I ask myself, "Will she know the difference between rape and sex? How should I explain the difference to her? Should I tell her what happened to me?"

A Message to the Readers:

Writing this story was very painful, but in the long run it has made me a stronger person. It has made me sure about myself.

Rape is never the fault of the person who is raped. It took me a long time to understand that Mr. Jones raped me and it was not my fault, but now that I don't blame myself, I am a stronger person for it.

The message that I would like to send off to you is this: if something bad has happened to you or anybody that you know, try not to let it put you down. Let it be an experience that will make you even stronger. And one more thing—never feel like you're alone. Other people may have had a similar experience and can understand you.

The author was 15 when she wrote this story.

Phillip Rollano

Haunted

By Anonymous

It wasn't my fault. That's what people say. Still, it haunts me every day. I wonder all the time, what did I do that made this happen? Does the fact that I was young mean I couldn't have prevented it? Maybe if I were smarter, I would have understood what was happening. I would not have waited three or four years to tell someone. I could have done something. I didn't stop him. I listened and did what he said. So I'm to blame. Right?

I was 8 years old the day I was raped. It was somewhere between the middle of spring and the middle of summer. It was a regular day. Cats were outside fixing their bikes and messing with firecrackers. I was at my babysitter's house and her son was watching me while she was out.

My babysitter's son was like a role model to me. He was 17, had friends on the block, girls, and was always nice. We would play fight. He'd call me his cousin and take me with him when he went to chill. I was a young boy basically growing up without my father, so he was sort of like a big brother to me.

The day it happened, he and I had just made some burgers and fries and were watching TV. I don't remember if we were talking or what we were watching or really if the TV was even on. I just know I was looking at it. When I was done with my fries I asked him if I could have some more.

He asked me, "You want more fries?" and I said, "Yes, please." So he told me that if I wanted more fries I had to do something. He told me to go in the bedroom and pull down my pants.

I went, only thinking about how I was going to get more French fries. I never have understood why I did what he said and I doubt I ever will. He came in the room and told me to look straight ahead. After that, I don't remember much. I never have been able to recall the pain. I don't even know if there was any. I just assume there was.

After it was over (in my mind it starts and ends at the same time), he gave me some French fries and told me he would kill me if I ever told anyone.

In the weeks after it happened, all I remember is watching *RoboCop* and not much else. I think part of the reason I don't remember much is because when something like that happens to you, you don't want to think about it, you just want it to go away, so your mind kind of shuts down. Besides, after it happened, I didn't talk to anybody about it, and when I finally did, they didn't have much to say, so it never seemed that real.

But after it happened, I made up some story to convince my mom to get me a new babysitter. After she did I thought it would be all over, but really, it wasn't. For a couple of years I pushed it out of my mind, but still it haunted me in other ways.

For one, my behavior changed from bad to worse. I was doing everything and anything that could be done with girls, except for the actual act of sex (my mom said if I did it I would burn in hell). I got kicked out of school for the last two months of 3rd grade. Plus, I started stealing.

My behavior wasn't all about the rape. I was already a little bad boy. But it did make me act even crazier. I acted in all sorts of wild ways without really knowing why, like I wasn't living my own life, like I was on autopilot, like I was watching myself on TV.

I never thought about the rape itself. I guess I had blocked it out so much that I didn't even remember that it happened. But in little ways it would come up.

I had a toy car that I had liked to play with which I had left at my old babysitter's house, and for years I bugged my mother about getting it back from there. It was the car from the cartoon *Bionic 5*. It was purple and yellow with missiles. I had it with me every time I went to that house, and sometimes I would leave it there. After, I would always think about how I lost my car in that house and I couldn't go and get it back.

At the time, I didn't understand what I had truly lost, or that the car was a symbol of something bigger—a symbol of everything that had been taken from me when my babysitter's son raped me. I just knew it was important and that I longed to have it back.

Then, when I was 10, I was just sitting down one day and everything flashed through my head and I realized I had been molested and that I needed to tell someone. I thought about everything I had done with girls and felt ashamed, because they hadn't fully understood what we had been doing anymore than I had. I felt I had become like him, my babysitter's son.

By then I was living down south with my father, so I went to tell my stepmother. I was scared, but I thought that since she was a psychiatrist she could make it go away. But all she said was that it wasn't my fault and then she let it drop. I left feeling even more confused. I felt dumb for even bringing it up.

Then when I was 11 and living with my mom again, I told her

what had happened. I had begun to have a lot of flashbacks of the rape and I could tell that my mom was worried. But when I told her, she and her boyfriend acted like I hadn't told them anything at all. I understood that it was four or five years after it happened, but she didn't even hug me.

She just said, "What you want me to do about it? It's too late now. You should have told me when it happened." I went to my room and cried. I felt that it must have been my fault if no one could or would help me.

After it was over, he gave me some French fries and told me he would kill me if I ever told anyone.

Soon I was thinking about it every day. I could just be walking and I'd remember it. It really didn't take anything. The worst was when I was 15. By then I had entered the foster care system, and I got into a scrape with three or four guys in my group home who started rumors that I was gay.

Every day I was approached by someone who had heard the rumors. I was afraid to go to sleep because one or two kids said they were going to sneak into my room and have sex with me. I had to fight people off and on until the whole thing died down. I was in a constant state of turmoil.

And in the background, always, there was my secret. Every day I would wonder, "Can people tell I was molested? Do I walk like regular cats or do people see a 'take advantage' sign on me?" I wondered, "Am I gay because some man molested me when I was 8?" After all, I took my pants off when he asked me to, didn't run when he did it. I was afraid it was my fault, that it was something I had wanted, something I made happen.

Even after the rumors died down, I continued to try to prove I was a man. I looked for trouble in the streets and talked to anything with a pretty face. I once hopped out of a car to get a girl's number because my uncle said she looked like something I should bag. But none of that made my fears go away.

Instead, the memories came back with a vengeance. Last year,

I was bugging out about something or other and staff restrained me. I started to get the signs I usually get before a flashback—which is when memories of that time come flooding back as if they were happening right then. I tried to get in control, but it was too hard with two guys holding me down. I started catching little spasms, so they held me tighter.

I tried to tell them to let go. I told them anything that came to mind. The staff wouldn't listen, and after a while I just remembered so much that happened that day I was 8 and I started shaking. Next thing I knew I was crying. I wasn't totally out of control yet, so I turned my head so they wouldn't notice. I was afraid that if the staff knew I had been molested, they would go and spread my business and crack jokes.

Finally, it all happened at once. The tears were running down my face and I was shouting, "You're not going to do that stuff again" and trying to fight them off of me. The staff called for an extra hand. One was at my feet and legs, one was sitting on my back, and one was pulling my wrist to my shoulder. Finally, I calmed myself down.

I told the staff to close the door and I told them what had happened. I felt pitiful. I was afraid to look the staff in the eye. I didn't want to tell them what had happened. The last nine years had taught me that it was better to hide it.

Nothing much happened, though, good or bad. The staff were cool. They got up and said they were sorry. I told them I understood they had to do their job, and that was that.

I still think about what happened almost every day. I walk around with a secret that I feel I have to hide. I know that lots of girls who have been raped feel that way too. But maybe guys feel it even more—like it has to be hidden so deep, like we have to hide it even from ourselves. If my parents had sat me down and talked to me instead of acting like it never happened, maybe I would feel less ashamed.

The feelings I've had all these years are so strong. I never saw my baby-sitter's son after my mom took me to a new one. I don't remember his name, and I doubt I would recognize his face. But once when I was 13, I tried to find him because I wanted to kill him. The thought filled my head every day for about three months. But I was too afraid to walk down that block where he lived.

Last summer I'd had a little to drink and I guess the liquor gave me the courage to confront my demons, so I decided to go there. I had stopped being afraid of seeing my babysitter's son. I was just afraid of the pain I might feel from the memories of the rape.

I walk around with a secret I feel I have to hide. I know that lots of girls who have been raped feel that way too. But maybe guys feel it even more.

But when I got to that block, I recalled other sorts of memories, good memories—my kindergarten graduation, old friends and family who used to live there too. It gave me a type of release to confront my fears. And so has writing this story. Life's got a screwed up sense of humor, but I guess I think that if I deal with the scars, one day they might heal.

Still, there's a part of me that doesn't know if I can ever fully deal with the rape. It always makes me wonder if someone's trying to take advantage of me. It makes me feel I've got a shameful thing I have to hide.

It's messed up that something that happened when I was 8 can still affect me so much now. It's messed up that someone can come into your life for so brief a time and screw everything up so much. I feel like no matter what I do, I can't get back what was stolen. But I'm writing this story because I also know that if I keep it hidden from myself, the abuse will only surface in more painful ways.

The author was 19 when he wrote this story. He later joined the Marines and ran a computer business.

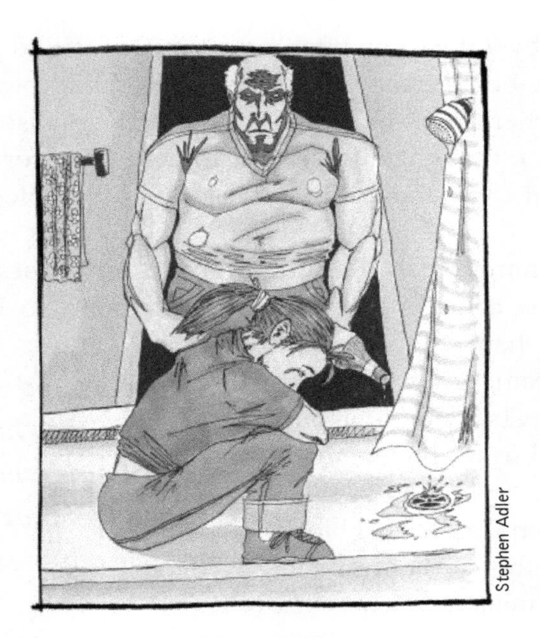
Stephen Adler

Family Secrets

By Anonymous

I can remember hiding in the bathroom when I was small, scared that my father was going to touch me in places where I did not feel comfortable. Some days when my mother would go out, I would lock myself in the bathroom until she came home.

I had a feeling that what my father was doing was wrong, but he always told me he did the things he did because he loved me.

I was around 7 years old when my father started abusing me sexually. He never stopped. I left the abuse behind when I entered the foster care system at the age of 12.

When I was growing up, my parents yelled at each other all the time. My mother would come out of her face and call my father a bald-headed bastard. I can remember my father coming home drunk and breaking all of the TVs in the house. It was hard for me to come home from school with my friends because I was scared that I was going to see my father drunk, yelling at the top of his lungs on some street corner.

Times were hard for me. I felt so bad inside. When my father was drunk my house was like a police station. Almost every day the police were at our house, because the people who lived above us complained about all the screaming they heard. When the police came, my mother told me to hide under the bed. She said that if they saw me they would put me away in one of the places that Orphan Annie was put in.

Once my father went after my mother with a knife, so my mother and I started sleeping in the bathroom so my father could not hurt us. It was hard sleeping in the bathtub every night. And he would still touch me when my mother was not around. The only thing I looked forward to was going to school and getting out of that house.

When my father was not drunk, and when we were out of the house, he was a bit of a different person. He would take me a lot of places, like different states and parks. Sometimes I felt funny being around him because, when we would go outside, he would be so nice to me. He would always buy me anything I wanted.

But the things that he got for me didn't make me feel any better. I wanted him to be a real father and not hurt me the way that he did. When he got me stuff, it didn't erase what was happening. It was like he was trying to buy my love.

Things got even harder for me when I hit the age of 10. At this time I stopped sleeping in the bathtub, because my father had started to get a little better. He was not as physically abusive as before, and he stopped drinking as much as he used to. But he was still touching me, and now I had to sleep in the same bed as him and my mother. Anytime I told my mother I wanted to sleep in the living room, she would tell me to sleep in the bedroom, because I was going to mess up the living room if I slept there.

I was scared that my father might try to do something while my mother was sleeping, so I barely slept at night. During the day, I couldn't keep awake in class.

My father's touches were leading into other things. My father was now raping me. I felt like I just wanted to die. I would sit down and cry for no reason. I would cry in school, church and my house.

And my mother was no support. She was always putting me down and calling me names. Two years before I told her I was raped by my father, she even wrote on the wall with red ink that my father and I were potheads, and that we were having sex together. That made me feel real bad. It made me feel that deep down inside of her heart she knew what was going on, and she did nothing to stop it.

I tried to stay away from home as much as I could. I joined the swim team, the basketball team and the softball team. I even tried soccer, although I didn't really like it that much. Sports took my mind off the abuse and kept me away from home.

I won an all-star award in basketball, but my mother wasn't happy. Instead she would say things to upset me like, "You need to lose weight," or "You could have done much better." My mother stopped making me dinner because she said that I looked like a big fat pig. So I was living off cereal and junk food that I would buy at the store.

All the time I was wondering, "Why me? Why am I going through all this pain?" I didn't expect things to change for the better. I knew that they were going to change for the worse. It didn't make any sense to me why it was happening.

In 5th grade we started learning a little bit about our bodies, and I was really coming to believe that what my father was doing was dead wrong. In school, we were learning that our bodies were our temples and that no one should abuse them. It made me sick to sit in class hearing that, and then think about all of the horrible stuff that my father was doing to me.

If only I could turn back the hands of time, I would not have let the abuse go on for six long years of my life. But I didn't say anything because it was like my father had some mind game put on me to make me believe he did those things because he loved me.

When I entered 7th grade, talks about sex came up a lot in and outside of school. The conversations made me uncomfortable. My friends would always talk about how they were going to have sex with someone real special, someone they might end up married to. I was upset that I was never going to have that special moment, and do it with someone real special.

Because my mother would not believe me, I decided to tell one of my teachers.

When the girls in my school would ask me if I was a virgin, it was hard to answer them. I told them that I was a virgin, but I really didn't know if I was. All I knew was that I did not want my father to do the things that he was doing. I always told him to stop. I would cry, scream, and try to push him off me. Nothing worked.

I felt like a big part of my childhood had been taken away. I felt so ashamed that I did not want to tell any of my friends about what was happening.

I couldn't take the pain anymore. I felt so dirty inside. I just wanted to kill myself. I even wrote notes to my friends about ending my life, but I never gave them to anyone. In my head I knew that death would not be the answer. Plus, people would have thought I was crazy. They had no idea what I was going through.

Around the beginning of January, I tried something new. I told my mother that my father had raped me a lot of times. It was hard telling her, because I had kept it a secret for so long.

My mother had a strange reaction. She got mad at me and said that my father would never do something like that. After that she said, "You better not tell anyone what goes on in my house."

That comment really hurt me. It made me believe that deep down she knew I was telling the truth, and still she wasn't going to do anything about it.

Because my mother would not believe me, about two weeks after I told her, I decided to tell one of my teachers who I was close to. I felt bad that I had to tell someone else when my mother should have been the one giving me support.

My teacher listened, and took action to get me placed in a better environment. That day I was taken out of my parents' care, tested for abuse and placed in the foster care system.

Even though I was now away from my parents, I was still very upset inside. My mother would call me every hour to tell me to take back that I said my father had raped me. I think she did not want to get my father in trouble because he was the one supporting her with his money.

But whatever the reason, my mother was hurting me a lot. I had just turned my father in for abuse, and I really needed to feel loved. Instead, my mother made me feel unloved.

I was also having a lot of bad dreams and flashbacks. It was hard for me to do anything without thinking about all of the things that my father had done to me. I got to the point where I couldn't deal with it anymore, so I stopped eating, and was admitted to a hospital.

When I returned, one of the staff at my placement knew what I was going through. She would pray with me every night. We prayed that I would overcome what had happened to me. She also invited me to church. I started to love getting up every Sunday to honor and praise the Lord. I started to feel better about myself when I was going to church. The only thing that was helping me at that time was my faith in God.

I did not trust any guys, and it was hard for me to talk to them. But when I turned 14, I started thinking about guys a little bit. I wanted to start dating and find someone to love me for me. I met a sweet guy who seemed very nice. He would always stop by my job and make sure I was fine. He also called me like five times a day.

In the back of mind every time we went out I would think he might just use me for sex. But he was not like that at all. He had good values. He also went to church on Sundays.

I had prayed that I would find someone like my boyfriend. I also had prayed for God to help me deal with being raped. Now it was as if He was answering my prayers. I was not even thinking about what happened to me that much.

Then one day I was with my boyfriend and we were kissing and hugging. I started to get flashbacks about my father. I pulled away from my boyfriend and started crying. Just when I thought it was over, the painful thoughts were coming back to me.

A few weeks later I told my boyfriend what had happened. It made me feel better telling him, because he is part of my life and I don't want to hide things from him. He understood and respected if I did not feel comfortable with him touching me in a certain way. That is what I really needed—someone to understand why I was feeling that way. That was over a year ago and my boyfriend is still a support in my life.

Still, it's hard dealing with having been raped. I don't want to have any flashbacks, but sometimes I still do. I also cry a lot, sometimes for no obvious reason. Other times I get very emotional and start crying when someone yells at me or curses me. I get teased a lot for my crying habits.

The abuse still affects me in other ways—sometimes if someone touches me and I'm not expecting it, I get upset and get an attitude. Sometimes I still feel alone and like no one can understand what I've been through.

But I try to put the past behind me, and try to make something of my life. I keep busy and think about the future. One day I want to own my own daycare center or be a lawyer. I also want to have a house of my own, with my husband and the three kids I plan to have.

The author was 16 when she wrote this story.

My Love, My Friend, My Enemy

By Anonymous

One afternoon about two years ago, when I was 14, I was at the gym working out and I saw a really hot guy. He was tall, slim, and clean-cut, and he gave me a deep, penetrating look.

A few days later I went back to the gym and saw him again. We started talking and it turned out he lived in my neighborhood. His name was Maurice. Eventually we started to go out.

He was just perfect for me. He was romantic and sweet and made me feel so secure. I remember one breezy night, late in the summer, we were walking around the neighborhood. He stopped to lean on a car, held my hands, and kissed me. He told me he really cared about me. I felt so good. My body tingled and my soul was floating. I had finally found a real guy who wouldn't be afraid to make a fool of himself over me.

For the next four months we laughed and shared some really good times. We went to the movies to watch Disney cartoons. We played footsie while we walked along hand in hand.

I got to know his family really well. Maurice met mine too and they were crazy about him. I used to go to his house after school practically every day and play around with his little sister. His mom was a sweetheart. His dad was funny, and his older sister—well, I loved her. She treated me like I was a real part of the family. On my birthday she brought me flowers. She called to wish me and my family a Merry Christmas.

People warned me that Maurice was a liar and that he would break my heart. My friend Calvin and even my next-door neighbor, Lydia, told me not to go with him. I just thought Calvin was jealous because he liked me, and Lydia, well, she thought she knew it all. I was so happy I couldn't imagine ever getting hurt.

When school started, Maurice stayed at his old school and I started at a new one. I had to adjust to a new lifestyle and make friends all over again. I changed the way I dressed and even the way I acted.

Where once I had been sweet and gentle all the time, I started acting bolder, tougher and more assertive. Maurice just couldn't understand. All he wanted was the sweet, innocent little girl he had once known. So we started arguing and arguing.

I still loved Maurice, but at the same time I found myself falling for Franco, a guy at my new school. It was one of the hardest things I ever had to do, but I told Maurice I wanted to break up. He was furious. We didn't speak for weeks.

But one day Maurice called and we talked. We started seeing each other again, but only as friends. He was a good friend. I felt even closer to him than when we were going out. Every time I broke up with Franco, I'd always run to Maurice for support. I could even call him up for advice in the middle of the night.

One time when Franco and I broke up, Maurice and I tried getting back together, but it didn't work out. I guess we were both too immature and stubborn.

One afternoon in November Maurice called me sounding gloomy. He said he wanted me to come over because he wanted to talk about "us." I felt bad, so I went over to his house. No one was home. Even his dog was outside. He took me down to the basement to "show me a drawing" he had made. The basement was filled with tools and weight-lifting equipment. Off to the side was a little room with a bed.

I remember thinking, "Please, God, please, let us make up." He took me to where the bed was. He started kissing my neck gently. I felt the way I used to feel when we first met—I felt loved.

Then Maurice started rubbing my breasts and I let him do that because I felt secure. It was so good being in his arms again. But, gradually, he started kissing me roughly, the kind of heavy kiss you'd expect from a crazed killer.

I told him no, to please stop, but he kept saying, "I love you. You know I won't hurt you. I missed you." Then he grabbed me by the arm, pulled me onto the bed and started pressing roughly against my body. I tried to scream, but he had the radio on so loud I couldn't even hear myself breathe.

I was so scared. I was screaming, "Stop it! Get the hell off me!"

All he said was, "Shut up, shut up!" He started to unbutton my fly and I tried to push him off, pull his hair, bite his arm, pinch him, but it was a lost cause. Then he pulled down my pants and started to push into me. I went into a state of freezing panic. I couldn't move or say anything. I was paralyzed.

When it was over, Maurice cursed at me. He walked to another part of the room and I made my move. I pulled my pants back on and ran as fast as I could.

That was the first time I ever had sex. It was horrible, and I felt I'd let him do it. I figured, "Well, I let him touch me and all, so he had a right." Now I know it was his fault, not mine. I was raped.

I cried all night (except when my mom was looking). When I finally fell asleep I had a horrible nightmare. In it, Maurice was on top of me again, but I managed to push him off. I grabbed one of his dumbbells, hit him in the head with it, and killed him. The dreams continue to this day. In some, I actually like having sex with him.

Days passed and I didn't tell a soul because I still thought it was all my fault. Then my friend Jason came up to me while I was walking home from school and asked me, "Why'd you have sex with Maurice?" He told me Maurice had started to spread rumors about how he had sex with me and that I "sucked in bed."

I couldn't believe it. Even after everything he'd done, it was still amazing to me that he could be such a low-life.

One time I walked past the local pizzeria and some girls I knew were standing by the corner. As I passed by they made comments like, "Oh, there goes the ho who had sex with Maurice." I just gave them a dirty look and kept on walking.

Days passed and I didn't tell a soul because I thought it was my fault.

Most of my friends believed the rumors too, and I started spending more and more time by myself. I even stopped communicating with my mom. She would constantly ask me what was wrong. "I'm just tired," I'd tell her.

My mother is a smart woman and noticed that I was acting different. I looked down most of the time and was starting to gain weight. Most importantly, I had missed my period. She knew that because I get very crabby and bitchy around the time I get my period.

I knew I should have told her what happened, but I figured she'd say that I looked for it. I didn't want to hear that. I needed support, not an "I-told-you-so."

I just thought I looked down because I was tired, that I was gaining weight because I'd eaten too much, and missed my period because I was stressed out. My mom, on the other hand, asked me straight up: "Are you pregnant?"

"How dare you think such a thing?" I told her. "Just because I'm quiet and fat, that means I'm pregnant?" To me being pregnant was having a special glow and getting morning sickness (which I didn't get). Besides, I thought that in order to get pregnant the guy had to cum inside of you and that didn't happen to me. I was so stupid.

My mom told me she had a dream with me and a baby and lots of blood. Dreams are very important to her. They are her way of predicting the future.

After a while I thought to myself, "Maybe I am pregnant." I felt my belly getting kind of hard, the way a pregnant woman's would. I thought about finding out for myself—just to make sure—but I wasn't sure where to go. My first thought was Planned Parenthood, but I was frantic. Where was it? How would I get there? I couldn't go alone—or could I?

And what if my mom found out? What would I do then? If I was pregnant, I decided, I didn't want to know. So, all I did was go to church every Sunday and pray that I wasn't.

One cold December day, my mom and I were on the subway on our way to visit family when all of a sudden she told me that we were going to see a doctor. I didn't want to see a doctor, but there was no way out.

At the doctor they did a urine test. I was scared, I mean really scared. What would I do if I were pregnant? What would my mother think? I remember saying to myself, "My God, my God, why have you abandoned me?"

When I was called into the doctor's office, I noticed a little pink box with a plus sign in the middle. It looked just like one of those home pregnancy tests I'd seen on TV. But I didn't know whether it was mine or not.

The doctor came in, looked towards the table where the thing was, and said she was sorry to inform me that I was pregnant. I looked at my mother and she looked at me. Tears of betrayal ran down her face, and tears of helplessness and anxiety came down mine. "It can't be!" I shouted, "Take another test!" I tried denying that I had had sex: "It's impossible! He didn't even cum!"

The doctor told me a story about a girl who got pregnant just by being real close to the guy. I couldn't believe this was happening to me. My mother demanded that the doctor check to see if I was really still a virgin, like I was insisting. The doctor checked and said no, that I had lost my hymen (that's the thin lining in your vagina, your "cherry").

My mom looked at me with pain in her eyes and right away told the gynecologist, "Take it out, right now." In other words, an abortion.

I couldn't say anything, I was in shock and I felt as if I no longer had control over my body. The nurse came over and stuck a needle in my right arm. "Don't worry," she said in a comforting, reassuring voice. Then I started to feel numb and was knocked out completely.

My mom would say things every now and then, like, "You're a slut...a disgrace."

I don't remember anything after that. I never found out what kind of an abortion I had, or whether you could tell if it was male or female. All I remember was being dizzy afterwards. I couldn't walk straight and was seeing double. I felt empty inside. I felt like I had committed some kind of crime. In a way, I think I had.

I was also petrified of what was going to happen once we got home. My mom yelled and screamed. She told my aunts and they were shocked. They couldn't believe I would sleep with a guy at such a young age. I wanted to tell them the truth but I thought, "Where's the proof?" I knew Maurice would deny it, so I didn't bother.

For months I kept it inside. My mom would say things every now and then, like, "You're a slut...a disgrace...so smart and so stupid at the same time...ingrate...this is God's punishment."

She would compare me to my cousin and friends of the family who she considered well-mannered and decent, a blessing to their families. What she didn't realize was that some of them were taking drugs and sleeping around.

Her cruelty and distrust drove us farther apart. I was forbidden to go out, wear makeup, use hairspray, buy new clothes, talk on the phone (unless it was about school work), watch TV or listen to the radio. I couldn't even answer the phone—she assumed the caller was one of my lovers or something.

I couldn't even go to school by myself, because she thought I would cut and meet my lovers (not lover, lovers). To this day, every morning, we take the same bus and the same subway. She told me that I won't be able to have a boyfriend until I'm in college. She won't let me go to my senior prom, no matter how well I do in school. And what hurt the most is she won't let me have the Sweet 16 birthday party I always dreamed of. You know, with the guys in tuxedos, the girls in their gowns—me in my gown—with lots of flowers and presents, dancing the waltz with my daddy, that kind of stuff. She said I didn't deserve it.

It started with Maurice. He took my virginity, he took my trust in others, he took me. I'll never be the same.

After that, my mom stepped in and took my freedom. As for my so-called friends, I had to live with their rumors and insults. Every little thing I had was taken away from me.

So many things were happening to me at once. I was having bad dreams. I was failing math (I had never failed a subject in my life). I was fighting with my mom. I was fighting with my new boyfriend Franco. I would fly into jealous rages, and he would complain that I wouldn't talk to him when I was either upset or angry or had something on my mind. I didn't know what to do. I wanted to kill myself.

I wrote a letter—more like a will—letting my mom know the truth, letting her know how much I loved her and how much I wanted her to be with my dad again (they have been divorced since I was about 4). I let my friends know why I had been so depressed and how I wanted them to remember me always.

I left the letter in a book, in the school locker I shared with my good friend Annie. She found it, read it, and came up to me and asked me what had happened.

I was mad that she had invaded my privacy like that, but I felt the time had come for me tell someone. I had to. Annie was very supportive, but she kept suggesting that I tell my mother. I couldn't do that, I just couldn't.

I told a few other friends too—partly because I wanted them to learn not to always trust guys, but mainly because I needed to get some kind of communication going so I could feel better about myself.

I learned what real pain is like, and how hatred for someone you once loved can ruin you inside.

Everyone who knew about my ordeal suggested I tell my mom the truth. I guess I will tell her someday. When, I'm not quite sure. But I will. Maybe when I get married or have a child. I don't want her to die without knowing the truth about the whole incident.

At times when I see a girl with a baby, I envy her. When I see TV shows about women giving birth, I envy them too.

My baby would have been born in late August or September. Sometimes I try to imagine how my life would have changed if I had kept it. Would I still be in high school? Would my friends still be there for me the way they are now? Would I still be living with my mom? Would I still be going out with my boyfriend?

I wonder what my baby would have looked like. Would it have been a boy or a girl? I know I would have loved the baby a lot, even though it wasn't conceived the way I would have wanted.

I still see Maurice around the neighborhood from time to time, and my bus passes by his house every day. I wish I didn't have to, but that's life. I don't look at him and he doesn't look at me. I'll be getting counseling as soon as I think I'm ready. I know it'll help a great deal.

I've learned a lot during the year since it happened. I learned what real pain is like, and how hatred for someone you once loved can ruin you inside. At times when I seem cheerful, I'm suffering inside—all because of one guy, one day and one nightmare.

The author was 16 when she wrote this story. When she showed this story to her mother, they were able to talk openly about what happened for the first time. She later graduated from college and earned a Masters degree in Spanish and Portuguese.

Melanie Leong

I Said, 'No!'

By Anonymous

Before I was raped, the most I had done with a guy was kissing, hugging and caressing. Then I would stop and their reaction would be, "Stop fronting." I wasn't fronting. I wanted sex to be special, and I wasn't ready to take on the responsibility of having sex.

I thought the first (or any) time I decided to have sex, it would be special and with someone that I loved. As for getting pregnant, I would be no younger than 25 years old and have finished college, have my own house, already be financially, emotionally and physically ready. But those were my dreams.

After I was raped, I felt ashamed. I thought it was my fault. Was this really rape? I looked up rape in many books and asked many people. I asked myself, "Did I give consent?" and my answer would always be, "No!"

I try never to think about details. But afterward I had nightmares about it happening again or even worse. I even thought about trying to kill myself. I thought of doing it every day, but I just couldn't.

I had it all—love, support, grades, and I had God in my life. What I wanted most was to just go back in time and erase this from happening to me.

Most of the time I try to hide my feelings from people and act cheerful, but at night I cry myself to sleep, all because Sean didn't listen when I said no. I thought rape wasn't done by someone you knew, but by a stranger, and he would have to beat you and leave marks on you. I had no marks but the ones inside. This wasn't a stranger, either. This was someone I knew.

One afternoon while I was going to Manhattan, I met a guy named Sean, who was tall and slim. I didn't glance at him twice because I wasn't interested in what he looked like or what he was saying to me, but then he began speaking to me about the Bible and religion. Me being in a youth group at my church and him saying he was 18, I decided maybe he could join. (My youth group ranged from 14-19.)

Then I realized I couldn't find my destination, and Sean said he lived close by, so he helped me find the place. I said, "Thank you," as he gave me his number.

During the next couple of days, we got to know each other over the phone a little. Sean called me and asked how school was, and said that he wanted to become a singer/rapper and that he worked.

I didn't like him as a boyfriend. He didn't have the body or the looks for me. I like guys with muscles and a clear face (Sean had pimples and he didn't look cute). Even so, I invited him to my youth group meeting and he agreed, but said he wanted to hang out with me first.

One day I decided to go hang out with Sean and tell him more about the group. At his house, I went and sat on the couch and got comfortable while Sean put the TV on and showed me around. Then I took off my shoes as he went to take a shower. I just watched *Days of Our Lives*.

He came out of the shower in silk boxers. I found it a little strange that he took a shower, but I didn't let it bother me. I thought maybe he wanted to freshen up; maybe he didn't want to smell in front of me. I had never been alone with a guy before.

But I didn't like him sitting there half naked. I told him to put on a shirt (his chest wasn't that nice) and he got mad and didn't. He didn't have a nice chest, but maybe I shouldn't have been so blunt.

Looking back on it, I think I felt that I could trust Sean, that I was in no kind of danger whatsoever. I found myself in a situation that was so new to me that I couldn't understand what was happening, and didn't know how to react.

Sean began complimenting me on my looks, clothing and the way I smelled. He was trying to guess what perfume I had on. Then he asked me to show him how to kiss. I looked at him funny. He tried to make his move. When I pulled away he began asking me if I knew how to kiss, but I didn't answer so he stopped.

When the soaps ended, he walked over to his bedroom and told me to come. I refused. He took my hand and brought me into the bedroom. Immediately he gave me a hug. Then he fell back on the bed while he was still hugging me tight. I told him to let me go.

He unhooked my bra. I asked him to fix it back. Instead, he rolled over and got on top of me.

That's when I knew it was time to go, but he wouldn't get off me. He pinned my hands down and began to kiss my chest with my shirt still on. I told him to please stop and he said, "Relax," then kissed me on my stomach and then my chest as he pushed up my shirt with his head.

All this time he was sitting on my stomach. I couldn't move. Then he let go of my hands and started to unbutton and unzip my pants as I struggled to keep them on. He asked me, "Do you think you're stronger than me?"

I didn't answer and 10 seconds after he said that he took off my pants. I knew I wasn't stronger, but I wasn't ready to lose my virginity, so I crossed my legs, asked for my pants back and slowly tried to move away from him.

He asked me where I was going. He started shaking me, moving me in different directions, asking if this is where I wanted him to put me. When he found a satisfying spot he wanted to put me in, he stopped shaking me.

The phone rang, so I started praying he would answer the phone while I got the hell out of there. But he said, "Forget whoever's calling. They'll call back."

I tried to get up, but when he noticed me moving he would move down and grab me by the legs and pull me down. I began cursing, saying, "Sean, stop f-cking playing."

He said, "Did I hurt you?"

I answered, "No, but I'm not waiting till you do."

All this time I was just shocked. I just didn't expect this at all. I thought that I could talk him out of it, that he would stop. I knew I couldn't beat him up and I thought if I fought him, he would get more mad at me and do something stupid. I didn't want him to hurt me or kill me.

I didn't want to lose my virginity, so when he tried to put it in, I said, "No," one more time and I started to twist and turn to let him know I was in pain. I wanted to scream, but no sound came out. I thought about taking the bed sheets and running out of the apartment, but I felt frozen. He didn't want to see how upset and scared I was. He just said, "Handle it like a mature adult."

I told him, "I can't, Sean. Stop. No."

Sean said, "Does your no mean no, or yes?"

"It means no," I said.

He said, "I knew you were going to say that. I don't know why I asked," as he proceeded to rape me.

I couldn't take it anymore so I told him it hurt, hoping he

would stop. When that didn't work I started crying. I thought he had gotten a little sympathetic and stopped, but when he got up I couldn't move. I just lay there crying.

"Are you going to get up?" he said.

I said, "Leave me alone," but I guess he didn't hear me, because he came and gave me a washcloth and said, "Wipe yourself." I asked why and he said, "Because I burst in you."

That's when I stopped crying. I started yelling at him, "Please tell me you're not telling me what I think you're telling me." At this point I stopped thinking of myself and what had just happened. I started thinking, "Please, God, I'm not pregnant by this bastard."

He told me maybe a shower would be helpful, thinking maybe if I'd stand up, pee or take a shower it might reduce the chance of me getting pregnant. I knew from books I'd read that this wasn't true but—damn, I wanted to jump off the roof if it would help, anything so I wouldn't be pregnant.

As I went into the shower he came in, too, but I didn't care. I just stood there letting the water make me feel a little better as he started soaping himself up.

I felt like I was in space as he asked if anything was wrong. I paid no attention. When he got out I didn't even notice until he came and asked would I like his towel or a fresh one. I said a fresh one, then I began showering my body with soap.

When I came out, I saw my clothes laid out nicely on the bed. I sat there thinking, "What the hell am I going to do?" He kept asking me if something was wrong but I wouldn't answer. There wasn't anything left to say. He knew what he did.

When I felt a little better I needed air so I went on his terrace and thought maybe I should jump, but the bars were too high. Then Sean came and said, "I know what it is, you're nervous around me now 'cause it was your first time." I just wanted to kick him.

Then he said, "What will your father do if you're pregnant?"

I said, "You don't want to know."

I decided to walk away, thinking I didn't want to talk about the situation anymore, thinking, "I'll just forget it ever happened, no one has to know and I'm not pregnant."

I thought it was a bad dream or something.

But it wasn't a dream. He wanted to rape me. He knew what he was doing and he just didn't give a f-ck about me or he would have stopped when I asked him to.

Then he took me to buy something to eat. When I wouldn't order anything he got mad, so I told him to buy me something to drink. I took like three sips and threw it in the garbage.

Then he started getting bold, asking what he looked like on a scale from 1 to 10. I said, "Seven," and he started saying he should get a higher number. I started ignoring him again. Soon we got to the subway where he also wanted to pay for my token. He put it in and made sure I went through.

I don't know what jumped into me, because the first subway I saw, I got on, not even sure if it was the right one, and all of a sudden I began crying when I realized I was on the wrong subway. I got off and tried to find the right one and it all came back, what had just happened. I needed to talk to someone.

When I got home, I took some pills thinking maybe if I could kill myself I wouldn't have to worry. I got to my senses, and then called my best friend. I told her what happened. She said, "Whatever you do, I'll be behind you."

That night I cried again. Then for the rest of the week I called Sean hoping he would tell me he was sorry or at least say that he didn't burst in me, but he didn't. We never even talked about what had happened, only that I might be pregnant, so he would always ask me if I was OK.

I went on with life, having nightmares, crying myself to sleep, and waiting for my period. I waited until a week after it should have come before I went to take a pregnancy test.

To have the pregnancy test I went to Ismal, a counselor I had met when I was working on a story about abortion. Ismal is prolife, meaning he's against abortion. His organization helps teenage mothers who have unplanned pregnancies and don't want to get abortions.

I had no one to talk to and I really felt comfortable talking to Ismal, so I set up an appointment with him. On the day of the appointment I felt sick and I was on the verge of canceling, but I couldn't—I had to take a pregnancy test.

When I got there, I sat on a couch and filled out a form. I was a bit nervous talking to him, but I began telling my story as if it were a riddle. I was too ashamed to just come out and say it. I avoided eye contact because I thought he could read the shame off my face.

I thought when you let a guy know up front that you don't like him, that would be it. I didn't think someone you knew could rape you.

Then he looked at me and said, "You know that was rape?"

I thought it was rape but I never wanted to admit it. I couldn't answer; it was as if the word was stabbing me—rape. That's a big, horrible, disgusting word. I bent my head 'til he said, "You need to press charges."

I said a sharp, "No, I can't."

The phone rang as he began to ask why, but I went to the bathroom to take the test. When I came out, there was a sense of friction in the room as we waited for the results. We talked about why I didn't want to press charges, and what the alternatives were if I was pregnant. I could have thought of a million places I wanted to be instead of there, because Ismal's questions made me feel emotional.

When he told me the test was positive, I felt like ice. I was speechless. The words I wanted to express wouldn't come out no matter how I tried. My mind just wandered as he tried to comfort me.

Ismal noticed and he told me it would be best if I went home and thought everything over and came back when I was ready to talk about it, which I did. After three weeks of thinking things over, I went back and talked to Ismal about being raped, but not being pregnant. Then I faced my fears.

I first called Sean, but could never get in touch with him, so I wrote him a letter and gave it to his doorman. It said that I was pregnant and to get in touch with me as soon as possible, but I never got a response. I don't know what I would have done if he had called; I was just scared and I was hoping for some type of miracle.

I want to talk about the rape, but to whom? I can't handle the burden, but I don't trust anyone, either.

Then I proceeded to tell my editor at Youth Communication, where I worked as a writer after school. She and Ismal were the ones who gave me the courage to tell my parents. That was the hardest thing, to tell my parents, and it was hard for them to believe it happened to me. I took so long to tell them. It happened June 20 and I told them August 15.

The day I told them, it was at least 80 degrees outside, but it felt like 20. I began shaking and my stomach was hurting. My parents were surprised, outraged and disappointed. After that, it wasn't my choice anymore what I wanted to do—they basically made me have an abortion and press charges. I couldn't say anything.

I always thought abortion was wrong. But I truly believe that Jesus forgives me due to the circumstances, and I must forgive the father of my baby, my parents, the doctor who performed the abortion and myself.

When I had the abortion I was shaking. I was cold and I felt like I could feel the baby moving. A man came and stuck a needle in my right arm as the doctor asked me if I had any questions. I said no, and a black woman with a bright smile came and said, "Hi, I'll be with you the whole time." Then I was knocked out, so I don't remember anything.

I was 10 weeks pregnant. I always wanted my first-born child to be a girl, so in my heart I believe she was a girl. I named her Essence, because she will always be someone special to me.

I remember hearing a woman's voice saying, "Wake up." I began to wake up as I saw a white sheet on me with a spot of blood.

I felt empty and began crying. A little later I went to the bathroom, and I felt a bit off balance. I sat on the toilet, and I suddenly vomited at least six times, one after another. When I had a little energy, I came out of the bathroom and sat down. I was surprised to see many girls who seemed fine and brave.

A nurse gave me a bag to vomit in and a cup of ginger ale with salted crackers. I finished it all, then vomited everything back up. I felt so drained. For the rest of the day, I just lay in my bed thinking about what had just happened and praying.

My parents also made me press charges against Sean. Even though I was afraid of having to tell my story in court, we went to the police and filed a report.

They found Sean and questioned him and he denied knowing me. When they said that I told them he raped me, he finally admitted to knowing me, but said that we never did anything.

They let him call me and taped the conversation. He apologized and he said he "wanted to work things out," and said, "I don't want to go to jail." He said he thought I was just playing hard to get.

The police did hold him in jail for a week, but that doesn't make me feel better. However much time he spent in jail can't change my past.

And at the time, I felt bad that he might go to jail because of me. I guess I was confused. I was shaking in the lawyer's office when he said Sean was arrested and in jail for a week.

In the end, though, they dropped the charges against Sean, because it was just my word against his, and they didn't have any proof.

But because we went to the cops, I got what most victims don't get, and that was a "sorry" from Sean, even though he didn't really mean it. He was just afraid of going to jail.

If I could say anything to Sean now, I would want him to know the pain I went through during the rape, after the rape, and how I've changed since then. The nightmares I endure at night, the tears I've shed when nobody's around. All the petty stuff of calling him names and cursing the daylights out of him—I don't want to do that, because it will never change what I went through.

For a while, I thought I could never deal with what happened to me. I thought death was the only way out. I couldn't understand. I think things happen for a reason, but I'm still trying to find out why it happened to me.

I also thought that either I was confused or Sean was, because after he raped me I was in total shock, but he acted like everything was normal and I was just acting insane. I think Sean knew what he was doing but he wanted to pretend it didn't matter.

But it mattered to me. It's been a year now, and being raped weighs on me still.

I still have nightmares. Often there's a light shining on a little girl saying, "Mommy, Mommy, I love you." I say, "I love you" back, and then I tell myself, "I love you, too."

Then the rape happens again. My dreams are usually true to the facts and that scares me.

I get mood swings. I flip on people for no reason. For a while I couldn't even remember what happened and that was good, but now I can't forget and I keep on having flashbacks. His face is in my dreams.

I try to do a million and one things to get everything out of my head, but I can't, and then I begin to cry when no one's around.

I work out most of the time, doing aerobics, and the exercise keeps me sane. When I exercise, I feel good about myself, I appreciate myself more. I like to keep my body in shape, strong and toned.

I still feel like my body is dirty, so I try and cleanse it and pamper it the best way I can. And exercising clears my mind and helps me feel relaxed.

I often feel angry and I get mad at the world. When I get an attitude with everybody, I grab a pen and write something to get it off my mind, or I cry myself to sleep.

Now, I don't even talk to people about the rape. I just keep it to myself. I stopped going to counseling, thinking I could handle myself. But I really can't. I try to stay calm and walk around with a smile, but I think I'm gonna crack. I want to talk about it, but to whom? I can't handle the burden, but I don't trust anyone, either.

Girls I know are always talking about guys and sex, and when they start talking, I just want to change the subject.

I don't like people feeling sorry for me. I want to be strong. For me to go through all this drama and bounce back, showing people I'm not weak, I'm not afraid, and they shouldn't be either—well, I admire myself for it.

But it's hard to keep a happy face. In my family, we never talk about the rape. We pretend it never happened. My parents can't handle the fact that I was raped and they think it was my fault. I don't want to talk to them about anything ever again. It hurts when your own parents blame you.

My parents are hard on me now and want to know my every move. They get mad at me if I'm even five minutes late, and they don't let me hang out unless it's writing for Youth Communication or going to school and church. The more my dad tells me what to do, the more I want to move out right after high school.

I also feel different from my friends, but I can't tell them why. Girls I know are always talking about guys and sex, and when they start talking, I just want to change the subject.

Guys and sex are the least of my concerns.

Sometimes my memories make me feel like I hate males—even though I know I don't—and I don't want to have any relationships with guys. I don't feel I could be comfortable and open.

I don't trust people, and I don't like to be touched. When someone touches me at all, I start shaking. Every time I shake I know something is wrong, and that I haven't gotten over being raped at all.

For a little while I started thinking that I wanted to become a lesbian and what would it be like? Would it be better? Or if I was with a white guy? I see a white guy in my dreams and he is sweeping me off my feet.

Obviously, I can't handle having a boyfriend right now, but I think I could handle one later on. Still, even then, I would only want to hang out at his house if other people were around.

I feel so much pressure to have a boyfriend and have sex, but I'm just staying away from all that. It seems like other girls in my school hate me because they think that I think I'm better than them, just because I don't want to do the cool stuff like have a boyfriend, have sex, drink or smoke.

I guess I am trying to keep control over my life now, by keeping to myself, working hard in school, keeping busy and staying away from guys. One of the scariest parts of being raped was feeling like I was powerless. Before, I could always talk my way out of a situation I didn't like. For the first time, I couldn't. I felt weak and scared.

I don't want to feel powerless anymore. Now I'm more aggressive and I speak my mind when I want something. Looking back, I wish I had fought for myself more.

When I became uncomfortable and didn't like what was happening, I resisted. But I wasn't experienced enough to know how to protect myself. When Sean gave me little signals that he wanted to have sex—like trying to kiss me, sitting close to me in his boxers, winking at me and pulling me into his room—I ignored them. I didn't want to sound stupid by asking him what every little signal meant. And I didn't realize I could be in danger.

I thought when you let a guy know up front that you don't like him, that would be it. I didn't think someone you knew could rape you. I kept telling Sean to stop, but he would say, "Why?" like it was a game.

I said, "Because I don't like it."

But he just said, "You don't know what you like until you try it," and pushed me further and further.

I said, "I don't want to do anything I will regret." I thought it was clear that I didn't want to have sex; I never thought he wouldn't listen.

The author was 17 when she wrote this story.

Melanie Leong

Scare Tactics

By Anonymous

Last year I planned to write an article about both sides of the abortion debate, so one day I went to a pro-life clinic called Expectant Mother Care (EMC), wanting to know more about their beliefs and what they do.

Before I went I was unsure about what abortion was or how I felt about it. I did not know what all the fuss was about. EMC advertises itself as being against abortion, so I spoke to a counselor there. What I found out was a little more than I could handle.

They believe abortion is wrong, so they try to scare teens into having their babies and they make it seem like it is easy to take care of a child. First they tell you the ways that you can get support during and after pregnancy. They tell you they'll give you a year's supply of baby products. Then they encourage you to switch schools to a high school for teen mothers.

Finally, they say they'll help you tell your parents, and if your parents kick you out, they'll help you move to a shelter for teen mothers. They act like you should be willing to give up everything in your life—your school and your family—to become a teen mother.

They also make abortion sound horrible. They take out an object that sounds like a baby's heartbeat. If you have the slightest thing called a heart, it makes you want to break down in tears.

They tell you horror stories about abortion (like that you'll die during the procedure) and show you a videotape of women having abortions. They told me these women were murderers.

They also gave me a million pamphlets about what happens to the fetus, about females who regretted having an abortion, and about teen mothers who had kept their child. One pamphlet struck me the most. It was called "Tragic Diary" and it went like this:

They tell you horror stories about abortion and show you a videotape of women having abortions. They told me these women were murderers.

October 5: Today my life began. My parents do not know it yet. I am small as the pollen of a flower, but it is I already. I will be a girl. I will have blonde hair and blue eyes. Nearly everything is settled already, even that I shall love flowers.

December 24: I am almost able to see, though it is night around me. When mother brings me into the world, it will be full of sunshine and overflowing with flowers. I have never seen a flower, you know. But more than anything, I want to see my mother. How do you look, Mom?

December 28: Today my mother killed me.

I couldn't believe what I was reading. I felt like this must be how the baby feels. I started to cry. I felt like I could not live if I had been this baby's mother, and I wondered how a woman could live with herself after having an abortion.

After I left, I was in shock. I felt sick. But I was also confused.

The EMC counselor acted like abortion is the worst thing in the world, but I still wanted to know the other side of the story. If it's so bad, then why is it legal?

I decided to educate myself by reading books and talking to friends and family about what they think. But that didn't help. Everyone was so against it that they couldn't even talk about it. By then I was pretty sure it was wrong. Still, I didn't think I had to make up my mind because I wasn't even having sex yet.

I thought, "These little girls are faced with such a big decision and all that lady can do is tell them her beliefs."

But things happen.

A few months later, I was raped. Because I had been there before, I went to EMC to have the pregnancy test—it was positive. When the counselor told me I was pregnant, he talked to me about keeping the baby.

He had some decent advice—when I told him that I wanted to go to a group home, he said it would be better for me to stay at home, and that I should tell my parents right away. He said that without my parents, I would feel like I had no support. But he was also clearly opposed to me having an abortion.

After that, I was so confused, but eventually I told my parents. At the time, I wanted to keep the baby. But when I told them, they forced me to have an abortion.

I was against it with full force. Not me, I could not, I would not. I cried every night. I wanted to be a mother, although I knew I was not ready to be one. I kept thinking about what they told me at EMC the first time I went: That I would die during the procedure and that, if I lived, I would be labeled a murderer.

When I went to the abortion clinic with my parents, I was shaking. In the recovery room, I spoke to other girls. They had so many stories about why they were there. Many said they had children already and they could not handle having another, and others said they didn't want any kids yet.

I felt a bit strange. They acted like an abortion was a common thing to do and so was sex. I thought to myself, "These girls need to use some type of contraceptive if they want to have sex." I felt angry at them.

Afterwards I was fine, physically, but I regretted having the abortion. I had seen the sonogram, and saw the baby inside, and I got so attached.

I did feel relieved not to have to be a mother. But I also felt shocked and sad—I felt like I had killed my child. It was only when I started school again, and realized how much I would have had to change if I had kept my baby, that I was glad I didn't.

After that, I knew I never wanted to have another abortion again. So even though I'm not having sex, I made an appointment at Planned Parenthood, where teenagers can get birth control for free, so I could go on the Pill and never get pregnant again.

When I went, I wished I had gone to Planned Parenthood in the first place. It's better to learn the facts about abortion and get counseling that helps you decide what you want for yourself—instead of getting scared at an anti-abortion place like EMC.

Almost a year later, I went back to EMC to talk to the counselor I had first met. This time, I saw two black girls in the waiting room. They were about my age. When I saw them, I felt outraged, because I knew the counselor was about to scare them just like she scared me.

She would make it sound like it's some kind of fantasy raising a child, even though she has no idea what a 15-year-old is going through or how her life will change.

I thought, "These little girls are faced with such a big decision and all that lady can do is tell them her beliefs, not try to help them make the best decision."

I wished I could have rushed those girls out of there and straight to Planned Parenthood, where they offer information and they help you form your own opinion. The counselors are there to help you make a decision, not to get you to do what they think you should do.

After all I've been through, I feel like I am finally sure of what I believe: that if you are faced with a situation where an abortion might be the best choice for you, then no one should stand in your way.

I don't believe that anyone can understand why females have abortions—unless they are faced with it themselves. If you think you can know your mind without having to face being pregnant and unprepared, then I think you are just fooling yourself. I should know.

I regret having to have an abortion, but it was the best thing for me at the time, and I am sure other girls who have had an abortion would say the same thing.

I don't think people who work in places like the EMC clinic can really understand the girls who walk in the door, and how it's going to change their lives to have a child. They don't care about what's best for the girl's life.

It seems to me that it's all about their religion and getting points to enter heaven. Once the girl has her child and they're both struggling—well, that part is not the counselors' problem.

The author was 17 when she wrote this story.

Arnel Sencion

Bye-Bye, Baby

By Anonymous

Not quite tall yet, but too big to be called small, his name is Gabriel. He has green and gold eyes, not mine but his father's. He has my smile, except for the dimples, which are all his own. He has red hair, more red than anything, that he hates to get brushed. He has real big ears that I tease him about, not to the point where I hurt his feelings, just to make him laugh. He likes to run and play fight. His mom thinks that he's too rough with me, but I tell her that I'm OK with it. I think little boys should be rough. He does too.

He's 3 going on 4 and already has a mind of his own. I'm proud to say that he got that from me. He tells me he loves me almost every time we speak, and if he forgets, he tells me twice the next time. I don't get to see him all the time, but when I'm at his house, he sleeps with me and holds me tight all night. He doesn't ever cry when I leave, but when we say goodbye he holds on just a little longer. I cry every time I leave him because I miss him when he's not near. Gabriel's my son.

When I was told I was pregnant with Gabby, I didn't have a place to live. I was on the streets because my mom had kicked me out—I can't remember the reason why. I had just been raped a month before. That's how I got pregnant.

Before I found out about Gabriel, I had decided to ask my mom if I could come back home. Finding out about the baby changed my plans. The home I grew up in was always full of screaming and hitting, and I wasn't about to let my baby live like that. Back then I didn't want my mom to know anything about him. I didn't want her to corrupt him in any way. I still don't, that's why she's never seen, heard or spoken to him.

When I hit my 8th month, Gabriel became really real. Until then I had made myself forget that he had a father who raped me.

After I found out I was pregnant, I ran away to another state. I had always had this thing for adventure. I wanted to be one of those teen girls who goes to some hick town, gets a job being a waitress, and makes just enough money to feed me and my baby and live happily ever after.

It didn't quite turn out that way. I did run away, but not to some hick town, and I did get a job, but not as a waitress. I went to Washington, D.C., and got a job I'd rather not talk about. I was living from place to place and the way my life was going wasn't how I wanted to be raising a baby.

Still, Washington wasn't all that bad, because that's where I met the woman who became my son's mom.

Kate took me in because I needed someone to care for me and she wanted someone to care for. I had seen Kate in my neighborhood once or twice before we actually stood face to face and talked. When she approached me, I thought she was crazy. She said I didn't have to pay rent or, as a matter of fact, do anything but live with her and let her take care of me. In my book, this lady was one of two things, crazy insane or a pervert. My money was on both. I told her, "No, thank you," and walked away.

But she came around almost every day for a month, bringing me things like juice and snacks and just talking to me. At first I worked really hard on not liking her, but in the end I gave in. Without her food, I wasn't eating. And by then I was showing a lot. I needed to get off the streets. I said yes. Now I think that was the right decision.

I was a crab during my pregnancy, but other than that things were OK. Then I hit my 8th month and Gabriel became really real. Not that he wasn't real before. It's just that until then I had made myself forget that he had a father who raped me. I hadn't thought about what he would look like if he didn't look like me. I kind of made myself believe that I made him by myself. But when Gabriel was almost here, one by one all my fears hit me in the head.

I talked to Kate about how afraid I was of being someone's mom. You see, all my life I had been told that the reason my mother beat me was because her mother beat her and so on. I wasn't ready to risk my son turning out like me just because I couldn't or wouldn't keep my hands to myself. I didn't know the first thing about being a mom.

It also scared me to think that I might not love my child because of what his father did to me. I didn't know how to explain to him that his father was a rapist. Even though that conversation was years away, the truth of the word weighed heavily on my mind and heart.

Ultimately, I didn't want that man's baby. I didn't want to be reminded of him every time I looked at my child. But that meant I didn't want Gabriel, and that made me feel ashamed.

I told Kate all that and more. She told me that I wouldn't be raising Gabriel alone. She would be there no matter what, and we would deal with any problems that came up when they came up. Still, I wasn't sure that was enough for me.

I began to think of asking Kate to raise Gabriel. I knew Kate would love Gabriel no matter what. She didn't know his father, so she wouldn't remember what it felt like to be hurt. She wouldn't look at Gabriel and see a rapist. Whenever she looked at him, she would only see Gabe and me.

Gabriel's father was white, and when Gabriel entered this world, he looked just like a white baby. He had pale green eyes and the little hair he had was bright red. Kate said that it would darken up, and it did, but not that much. He really didn't show any characteristics of being mine. That made me even more sure that I wasn't ready to raise Gabriel.

I told Kate what I wanted. She had no problem with taking care of Gabe, but she did have a problem with me running away. We decided together that I would stay for a year, and if I still thought that leaving was a good idea, we would decide what was best for Gabriel then.

That year I learned a lot, like how it feels to be truly tired. I learned how it feels to be really afraid of hurting someone smaller than you. It wasn't because he was new, it was because he was mine. I had taken care of kids almost all my life, but never any who depended on me like Gabe did.

The first three months of Gabe's life, he slept with me. I remember staying awake almost every night worrying that if I fell asleep I would crush him or that he would fall off the bed. During that year I came to love Gabriel. After a while, I could see that he not only had my smile but also my independent attitude.

But that year was also really hard. I had too much stuff in my head that needed to be cleared out. I needed time to face my ghosts. I needed space for myself.

I don't know how to explain what I was feeling or how much I needed to get away without you believing that I didn't love my little boy. Because I did, do and will always love Gabriel. I know no matter what I say, people still may think that I didn't love my son and that's why I left him, but they're wrong.

I decided to leave because I was too afraid and unprepared to handle that responsibility. And because that's what I do. When a place gets too familiar, I feel closed in, and then I need to make a move, to get some breathing space. I couldn't make Gabe live like that. I didn't want to.

At one point I did think about taking him with me, but I had no money, no home, no way to feed him. I didn't have one good reason to take him from his home. The only argument I had was that I loved him and wanted him with me, but that didn't stand up too well in the court in my head. Loving him meant I wanted the best for him (food every day, a warm place to sleep, a stable environment) and I couldn't give him those things at that moment in time. (I still can't.)

Kate could. I had seen her with my son. She was patient with him, played with him, read to him. And the way she talked to him made me sure he would grow up to be a smart kid.

The night I told Kate was long. Gabriel was there. He was only a year old, so he didn't understand much, but he held my hand the whole time and listened. A lot of promises were made that night. Kate made clear that I was to always call when I needed something and that I was to come whenever I could. I explained to my baby that I loved him and that I always would, and that just because I wasn't living with him didn't mean that he wouldn't see me.

I know no matter what I say, people still may think that I didn't love my son and that's why I left him, but they're wrong.

I know he doesn't really understand, though, because from time to time he still asks why.

It's been almost three years since I left Gabriel. I talk to him every week, but I only see him a few times a year. That's not enough, but it's enough so that he doesn't forget me. I miss being there for his birthday and other occasions, and I miss being able to just get up in the night and watch him sleep. But knowing that he's being loved and taken care of every day by someone I love and care for makes it easier to bear.

Instead, I get to be young and make mistakes. I'm glad that I met Kate and that we have the relationship that we do, because otherwise I wouldn't get to see Gabe grow up and he wouldn't know me while I'm growing up, too. It's important for my son to know that I love him. I tell him that every time I talk to him, and Kate tells him too. But it's also important for him to be in a stable home where he can get the love he needs, every day.

He's not quite tall yet but too big to be called small. He has green and gold eyes, not mine but his father's. He has my smile, except for the dimples, which are all his own. He has red hair, more red than anything, that he hates to get brushed. And real big ears that I tease him about, not to the point where I hurt his feelings, just to make him laugh.

His name is Gabriel and he's my son.

The author was 19 when she wrote this story.

Stephanie Fulcher

Done Wrong

By Anonymous

When I was 15, I was the victim of a gang rape.

My biggest mistake was not calling the police. I couldn't bring myself to do so because then my family would know and they were the last people in the world who I wanted to find out.

My second biggest mistake was staying with the guy who allowed this to happen to me.

I was in 10th grade when I met Damien. I was getting into my buck wild stage, when I didn't care about anything in the world except myself.

School wasn't very important to me. I would only go for attendance and then leave with some of my friends. At home, I didn't get along with anyone because it felt like they were all against me. I was alone in my little world and only my friends could understand me.

A week before winter vacation, I was walking down the block with two of my friends when a guy just stopped me and we started talking. I was dealing with other guys so I figured he would just be a new addition to my list.

But during that first conversation, Damien kept saying all the things that I wanted to hear, like "You gonna be my shorty on the real," and "You wifey material, so I ain't gotta look no further 'cause we gonna make it happen." Mind you, we had only known each other for about half an hour.

When I ran into the guys who raped me, they would always have some dumb-ass smiles on their faces, like everything was as cool as a glass of Kool-Aid.

I separated from my friends and stayed with Damien. We were going to his house when he realized that he had let his brother hold his keys. We had to wait in the building until his brother came back. While we were standing in the hallway, he pulled his willy out and asked me a bunch of sex-related questions.

At first this really grossed me out and kind of pissed me off. I knew I was worth more than a five-minute thing in the hallway. But nothing like this had ever happened to me before and I really didn't have a clue as to how to handle it, so I stayed quiet.

"You talk on the mike?" he asked. At first I didn't know what he was talking about, but it soon dawned on me that he meant oral sex.

"No," I answered.

I was nervous as hell and I wanted to go home, yet I also wanted to be with him. He had looks to die for. His face just kept me there. I had never seen anything finer than him. He was around six feet, had a caramel complexion and just had it goin' on.

"Shorty, why you frontin'?" he asked with a real cocky attitude. He zipped his pants back up, finally.

"I'm not," I said. "I just never did it and I don't plan on doing it either."

"Well then...let me eat you out," he said.

My eyes popped wide open. I was so surprised that he said something like that. Many guys would back away from giving oral sex to a girl, but I guess he figured that if he could get me open any way possible, then I would be an easy lay.

I'd had sex with two guys before that, and those two almost needed a crowbar to pry my legs apart. I mean, I would get horny during foreplay, but when it came down to actually having sex, my body wouldn't be in an excited state anymore, so it was kind of boring.

"Not here," I said. I knew that I didn't know Damien long enough to even give him a peck on the cheek. But I did want to see him again.

I went home and he promised to call me the next day. I was happy knowing that something as cute as Damien would be mine. I would think to myself, "Damn, he wanna get with me so bad that he wanted me in the hallway."

A week passed and I didn't hear from him, so I decided to call him myself. When I called I was kind of hurt because he didn't even remember who I was. It took him a while to figure out where he met me. After he remembered, I felt better. I thought that we could progress into talking about us.

I was so hooked on him that I would do anything just to see his face. We made plans to meet again during a school day.

I went to his house early in the morning a few days later and almost instantly he tried to take my clothes off. I wanted him too, but I didn't plan on having sex with him so early. I thought that we were just going to chill, watch TV or listen to music.

Even though this was only the second time I was seeing him, I just had to know what such a beautiful body like his would feel like. He definitely had me in a trance. We had sex for a number of hours and I loved every minute of it. For the first time I could actually say that I enjoyed having sex.

Then there was a knock at the door. While he went to answer it, I put some cover over myself and waited for him to come back. The next thing I knew, three of his friends were in the bedroom. I had this feeling in my stomach that something wasn't right.

"Damien, can't they go in the living room or something? I'm not dressed," I said.

When I looked in his eyes, I knew that something was going to happen. Usually a guy wouldn't want his friends to look at his girl, period. So if he was letting them in the room while I was assed out naked, something was dead wrong.

"Nah. Chill, shorty. I got this, don't worry," he said.

As his friends started pulling down their pants, I got up with the sheet wrapped around me and started searching for my clothes. The only thing going through my mind was getting the hell out of there before they got up in here. I put on my underwear and tried to put the rest of my clothes on.

"Shorty, where you think you goin'? Come here, Ma," one of his friends said, taking off my bra and playing with my breasts.

I felt tears running from my eyes. There was nothing I could do. I tried to push them away but there were too many and they were too powerful against me. They pushed me on the bed and started what was to be the worst time in my life.

The pain was so unbearable. They had my arms pinned so I couldn't move and my wrists were feeling sore. Every time someone entered me, it was a forceful entry that felt like fire. Almost all of them had their turn despite my pleas for mercy.

Damien watched the whole time. Even though my eyes were filled with tears, I could see him smoking and resting on his dresser. He was watching as if it was just a regular porno flick on TV. I felt so disgusting and dirty.

After it was over, I passed out. I woke up alone in Damien's bedroom. I put on my clothes and left as fast as I could. I didn't get far because he was in front of his building smoking a cigarette.

"Oh, so you ain't got nothing to say?" he asked me in a harsh tone.

"What should I say to you? Do you know what you did to me?" I felt tears in my eyes.

"What you mean, what I did to you? How could you bless my men like that?"

"What? You saying this is my fault?" I felt like slapping the holy hell out of him.

"What, you tryin' to say you was raped? Shorty, do not play yourself like that."

The argument was escalating and we were both beginning to shout. I didn't want anyone knowing about what just happened.

"You know what, forget you," I said. I walked away, hoping to never see him again.

He called me the next night, apologizing and begging me to stay with him. It's hard to explain why, but even after all that happened I couldn't stay angry with Damien.

Although I feel that my boyfriend would never do anything to hurt me, I still get a "trust no one" vibe every now and then.

I was deeply infatuated. I wanted to be with him. It didn't even cross my mind that the whole thing could happen again because I didn't care. Too many family problems were erupting at home and I felt like I needed him.

Whenever I called him, he never rushed me off the phone, although it's not like he paid that much attention to me, either. I was like a big stupid cat, and he was the mouse that was always out of my reach. He only kept in contact with me to see if he could get me to go to his house. And of course, I went. I only had sex with him to make him happy, because if he was, then I was happy.

I would run into the guys who raped me from time to time when I was going to see him. They would always have some dumb-ass smiles on their faces like everything was as cool as a glass of Kool-Aid. I felt scared and pissed off every time I saw them.

Even that didn't interfere with my desire to be with Damien. The fact that he wasn't there for me while I was being raped and that he had probably set the whole thing up were things that didn't enter my mind. I didn't want to think of him in a negative way because I didn't want to push him away.

Looking back, I can see that what I did was wrong. I should have stayed away from Damien like Adam and Eve should have stayed away from the apple.

It's sad to say, but I don't think that I loved myself until after this happened. I always put other people before me and I guess I just forgot about including myself on the list of people who matter the most to me.

It took me almost two months to realize that Damien was not worth my time. I guess I finally saw the light when I heard the song "Silly" by Taral Hicks. The words that stuck with me were, "You're just a lover out to score, and I know that I should be looking for more. What could it be in you I see, what could it be? Oh, love, love stop making a fool of me."

I stopped calling Damien and didn't return any of his phone calls. After a while, he got the picture.

After it was over, reality settled in. I realized that I'd been taken advantage of and played for a fool. It felt like I was a puppet and someone else had been controlling my mind and my soul. I kept wondering, why was I so infatuated with this guy? He had done me wrong in the worst way and all I thought of was being with him.

I was depressed about the situation for a while. I would stay in my room for hours at a time and keep to myself. I stayed away from guys, which wasn't really normal because I wasn't shy and I did love attention from the opposite sex. But now I had a hard time trusting anyone.

I still see Damien sometimes because he lives near my school but I try to keep contact with him to a minimum. Whenever I see him, my blood starts to boil and I get so pissed off I can't even see straight. I deeply despise him now. The whole rape scenario replays in my mind constantly, and it hurts equally that he tried to make it seem like I wanted it.

It took a while but I think I have finally come to terms with what happened to me. I know that things I have done in the past were wrong. I know that things that were done to me in my past were wrong. It happened, and there is no point in trying to change it or cover it up.

If I had the self-esteem back then that I have now, I wouldn't even have acknowledged Damien's existence. I can gladly say that I do not have anything to do with Damien anymore.

I feel in control of my life again. I have become more focused on my schoolwork. I'm a senior and I'm in a college prep program. I work, volunteer and have many activities.

I always put other people before me and I guess I just forgot about including myself on the list of people who matter the most to me.

I do the things I do now because I want to be involved in programs that help people my age and younger. I don't want them to have to travel the road that I have already been down.

I also have a boyfriend who I care about very deeply. I've been with him for about two years now. He has become my best friend more than anything. He was actually the first person I told about this.

There were plenty of nights when I would cry on his shoulder, and sometimes I still do. He was very understanding and he let me know that I had done nothing wrong.

Although I feel that my boyfriend would never do anything to hurt me, I still get a "trust no one" vibe every now and then. My guard is up almost 100% of the time.

My boyfriend has done a great job of putting up with me and all of the things that put me on the down side. He is a great pick-me-up.

What I've learned from all this is that happiness is within yourself. If you don't love yourself, nobody else can do it for you. Wasting all of that time trying to please Damien was pointless. I should have spent all of that time and effort on myself.

Relationships like the one I had with Damien are so common, but girls don't like to talk about it because it makes them feel low. I hope some of them read this article and realize that they don't need a guy to make them happy.

Damien gave me some happiness. But with the happiness came a hell of a lot of heartache. And it just wasn't worth it.

The author was in high school when she wrote this story.

D. Alen Michailov

Putting the Pieces Together Again

By Mimi Callaghan

Whenever my friend Lisa is with her boyfriend, she is afraid that she might be trembling without realizing it, or crying without even knowing it, for a reason she would like to forget.

Late one night in November 1996, Lisa was raped in the Sheepshead Bay area of Brooklyn. Sometimes Lisa doesn't think she will ever get over the trauma of being raped.

That cold night, Lisa went walking to her aunt's house after getting into an argument with a friend who lived only a few blocks away. Suddenly, a large Asian man came out of nowhere.

"Are you lost?" he asked her. Before she could answer, he grabbed her and put an eight-inch knife to her throat.

"I really didn't think it was happening," said Lisa, 17. "When he grabbed me I remember screaming for God to help me. I figured that if he existed, this was his time to prove himself. As it happens, he never proved himself."

The man robbed her of two dollars. Then he dragged her into a driveway where he pressed the knife hard against her chest and forced her to take her tights down. He put the knife to her neck and sodomized and raped her.

"I went completely numb. I pretended this wasn't happening," Lisa said.

Lisa truly believed that she was going to die that night. She said that she was waiting for the moment when he would stab her. She braced herself for the pain, but it never happened.

One family member said to her, 'Well, what do you expect being out so late on the street by yourself?'

When the man ran off, she ran up the driveway and frantically banged on the door of the house. The couple who lived there called the police, who arrived in minutes. The police took Lisa to the station and called an ambulance while they asked her a few questions.

Then Lisa was taken to a hospital. She stayed overnight and her family was contacted. One of the police officers also stayed with her until the next morning.

When she came home, it seemed like her whole life had changed.

Lisa had never exactly had a close relationship with her family, and this seemed to drive them further apart. They told her it was nothing to worry about, and she would get over it eventually.

And sometimes her family seemed to blame her for what happened. One member of her family said to her, "Well, what do you expect being out so late on the street by yourself?" That made her feel as if she was asking for it.

They would also tell her how upset they were about the rape, but they didn't ask how she felt, even though she was the one who went through hell. It seemed like no one cared about how upset, depressed and angry she was.

Lisa would constantly replay the scene in her head, thinking, "Maybe if I fought him off more I would have gotten away, or he would have killed me and I wouldn't have to live with it."

But Lisa didn't want to believe that she lived in a world "where being a girl meant you had to be confined to do certain things, be at certain places only at certain times," Lisa said. "I didn't think traveling by yourself at night meant you were asking to be raped."

After she was raped, Lisa was scared to leave her own house or travel alone. Even now, if it is dark, she has someone meet her at the subway station to walk her the five blocks to her house.

When she is walking by herself and she hears the slightest noise, a twig snapping or footsteps that are only in her head, her heart starts racing, her chest pounds and she starts breathing heavily. Lisa is always afraid that it will happen again.

She also fears that she will see her attacker in the street. But what scares her the most is that the incident could take over her life, which is the last thing she wants.

About a month after she was attacked, Lisa started school again only to find out that everyone knew what had happened to her.

"I was the hot gossip," said Lisa. "I was whispered about, pointed at and so on. I was known as the girl who was raped. I was no longer known as me."

Two of her friends were supportive and treated Lisa as they always had. They didn't bring up the rape unless Lisa wanted to talk about it. And when she cried, they would be there to listen to her and comfort her. At a time when she felt extremely isolated, these two friends really helped.

But some people's reactions made her feel even worse. Months after the rape, a friend of hers kissed her. Then he jumped back, asking if she had gotten an AIDS test.

Things like this made Lisa feel like no one ever thought about what she was going through—how she would sit up and cry all night because she had to fake a smile and pretend to be happy.

How she wouldn't sleep for days on end, and when she finally fell asleep it was only for a few hours. Then she couldn't make it out of bed, but just lay there for hours.

She was immensely depressed and rarely ate. Instead she would smoke two packs of Marlboros a day. Sometimes she wouldn't talk at all. Other times she wouldn't get off the phone because she felt so alone.

In February, Lisa stopped attending school for the rest of the year. Then she didn't do much but hang out with friends who no longer went to school and wander around or visit her friends at college.

When they went to their classes, she'd sleep in the hallway. She didn't sleep at night anymore because of nightmares.

When her family realized that she wasn't going to classes, they tried to force her to go. Her parents said that she was just using the rape as an excuse for all her problems. She gave up on them after that.

Lisa attempted to start getting back into relationships three months later. She fooled around with a guy one night. She was petrified and trembled when they kissed.

Lisa didn't want a relationship at all, she just wanted to see if she could deal with kissing a guy, letting him touch her, letting anything happen. He didn't know what had happened to her, why she was trembling.

When he kept asking her, "Why are you trembling?" she felt bad, like she was using him. Afterward she hated herself for fooling around with someone she didn't care about. But in a strange way, she just wanted to see if she could be intimate with someone again.

Lisa got back into a sexual relationship about three months after that, but not before she took an HIV test.

If she was to come out HIV-positive she would never start up a relationship, she said. But the two HIV tests she took came out negative. She had never been so happy in her life.

When Lisa started to have sex again, she really didn't care about herself, she just wanted her memory of the rape out of her head.

"It was now or never, I thought to myself," Lisa said. "What was I supposed to do, let this guy plague my mind, take control of my life? He took a part of me that I will never get back, something I can't explain"

Even though Lisa didn't feel like she had a real relationship with the guy she slept with, she felt like it was something she had to do. Part of her just didn't want to flip when people touched her. She didn't want to see the rapist's face constantly in her head.

When Lisa is walking by herself and she hears the slightest noise, her heart starts racing, her chest pounds, and she starts breathing heavily.

"In some ways I feel as if this was my way of showing myself that I was OK, that I was normal," Lisa said. "And I know that it is not healthy for the most part, but in my case it helped me. It also hurt me and tore me up a bit, but this was my first step into saying goodbye to my fear."

The relationship didn't last long, only about four months. But in a strange way, it helped Lisa get over her fears of being touched. But emotionally he had also hurt her, and when they broke up, she felt even more distant and distrustful of people.

Still, when some time had passed, Lisa met her current boyfriend, and she has been able to have a relationship with him for the past seven months.

While the relationship is pretty healthy, Lisa said she sometimes can't go near her boyfriend or get intimate with him. Other times she will cry during sex.

After she was raped, Lisa felt like she couldn't trust anybody. It made her not want to care about anything or waste her feelings on anyone again. She doesn't think she can ever be the person she was before.

Her boyfriend knows how she feels and tries to help her deal with her emotions, but Lisa feels like he can never really know what it is like to be her and how she feels day to day.

But her relationship with him has shown her that she can still have feelings for other people, and that there are some people she can trust. Lisa knows she doesn't have to feel depressed and angry all the time. She can feel positive sometimes, too.

Still, she often gets depressed. It's hard to cope with all the intense feelings she still has. And she can't be by herself for very long. Lisa has flashbacks of the rape every now and again, although they're not as bad as they used to be. Even though they hit her hard and come out of nowhere, she tries to pretend they are not happening. And she still has nightmares sometimes, which set her back in getting over the rape. In many ways, it still haunts her.

Even though Lisa didn't have much counseling herself, she recommended that other rape victims talk out how they feel. She believes that it really isn't healthy to keep what you feel inside.

"I haven't been down that block where it happened; I always find my way around it. I am scared to know what would happen if I did. I think it would all come flowing back, and I am scared.

"I would see the house he took me by, the driveway he dragged me into and the wall of the house he raped me on. I would be able to give you every detail then, from where I was positioned to where I dropped my bag, to everything he did. Most of it is forgotten, but if I were ever there, it wouldn't be forgotten."

Even though Lisa didn't have much counseling herself, she recommended that other rape victims talk out how they feel. She believes that it really isn't healthy to keep what you feel inside.

This September, Lisa went back to school and because she

doubled up on classes, she will be graduating on time. She can't truly block out the rape or pretend it didn't happen, but she is trying to move on as much as she can.

"It is something that I went through that will forever terrorize me, but I can't change it," Lisa said. "It is something that I will always have to live with."

Mimi was 17 when she wrote this story.

Elizabeth Deegan

Recovering from Rape

By Mimi Callaghan

Survivors of rape often do not know how to handle their feelings about what has happened to them. Victims should know that there are people out there who want to help them—people like psychologist Patti Feuereisen.

Dr. Feuereisen counsels teenage girls who have been raped or sexually abused. When I interviewed her, she had a lot of information and advice to offer.

First of all, she said, a rape victim should go straight to a hospital after the attack. Most hospitals have a rape crisis unit. Hospitals also have counselors who can help rape victims deal with their feelings.

Dr. Feuereisen said it is extremely important to talk to someone, whether it's a counselor, a best friend or a parent. Talking about what happened can help victims deal with their feelings of terror, shame and humiliation.

"Rape survivors have different reactions. Some girls go into denial, they make themselves believe that nothing happened to them. They block it out. Now this can be very dangerous," said Dr. Feuereisen. "They could have a delayed reaction about a year or more later when something reminds them of what happened."

Many people who have been raped believe they will never get over the trauma. But Dr. Feuereisen said that teenagers who have been raped and who talk out their feelings can expect to feel happy about their lives again within a few years.

Some people believe that one type of rape, either date rape or rape by a stranger, is more traumatic than the other. This is completely untrue, Dr. Feuereisen said. Each is a violation and has its own trauma and problems.

In cases of date rape, the girl often feels responsible or guilty. Victims of date rape may blame themselves for being drunk or high, or they may feel like they led the guy on by being flirtatious. But these things never make date rape a girl's fault.

If a girl feels guilty, she often doesn't want to talk about it or deal with what happened. Sometimes date rape victims even stay with the guy. But it is important for all victims of rape to talk about it and get support.

Dr. Feuereisen also suggested that when girls go to parties, they take steps to decrease their chances of getting raped.

They shouldn't be drunk or stoned alone. If they want to get some play, that's fine, but girls should make it clear where their limits are. For the guy, getting some play might be going all the way.

"Girls need to band together and watch out for one another. If you're going to get drunk and stoned, make sure you have a friend who is clean that is going to be looking out for you," Dr. Feuereisen said.

When a girl is raped by a stranger, she tends to feels less guilty and she is more likely to go to counseling.

Stranger rape causes girls to feel anxiety and panic states in everyday life. They are often scared of the subways, they have nightmares and tremors, and they're afraid to go outside.

Girls who have been raped can have trouble sleeping, and they can get so depressed they eat too much or not at all. Eating disorders may develop. Often their grades take a dive.

Guys can be raped, too, and sometimes it can be harder for them to admit it, because they think rape only happens to girls.

But if a guy is raped, he needs help, too.

Victims of incest should also seek help. Kids who have been sexually abused suffer from many of the same problems as rape victims, Dr. Feuereisen said.

Talking about what happened can help victims deal with their feelings of terror, shame, and humiliation.

And incest can be even more traumatic, because an older person whom you trust is victimizing you.

"Sometimes when a girl is younger and she is molested, later on in life she doesn't know how to say no to sex. Incest survivors often become promiscuous. This could affect her throughout her adult life," Dr. Feuereisen said.

In Dr. Feuereisen's opinion, a girl who has been raped or sexually abused should see a female counselor and should receive interactive counseling, where the girl and the counselor both talk.

"Survivors should not be afraid to talk about what happened. Sometimes they are afraid or ashamed and some are scared to relive the incident, but some have to relive it every day. It is OK to think all these things," Dr. Feuereisen said.

She also recommended group therapy. That way the girls know that they are not alone.

She suggested that victims should be open with what happened to them because it will make it easier for them later on.

However, she warned that they will probably get some negative criticism from people who don't understand what happened. In cases of date rape especially, some people will say you deserved it somehow.

Girls also have to realize that being raped or molested might affect future relationships. Girls may feel afraid to trust a partner and may fear physical pain during intercourse.

Rape victims have trouble feeling comfortable or being able to get excited by physical intimacy. This is because the body can shut off natural responses that happen during intimacy. Dr. Feuereisen said it takes time and work, but victims will get over it and get back to normal.

"I see rape as a scar or wound that has just been cut open," Dr. Feuereisen said. "When it opens, it is vulnerable. When it is sewn up it takes a long time for the flesh to heal. You can always feel the scar, always feel something. You will feel it less and less even though you know it is always there. But you will get over it."

Getting Help

If you've been raped and need someone to talk to, you can call the Rape, Abuse and Incest National Network (RAINN) sexual assault hotline at:

1-800-656-HOPE (4673)

The hotline is free, anonymous and confidential, and it's available 24/7. You can also talk to someone online through their website: www.rainn.org.

FICTION SPECIAL

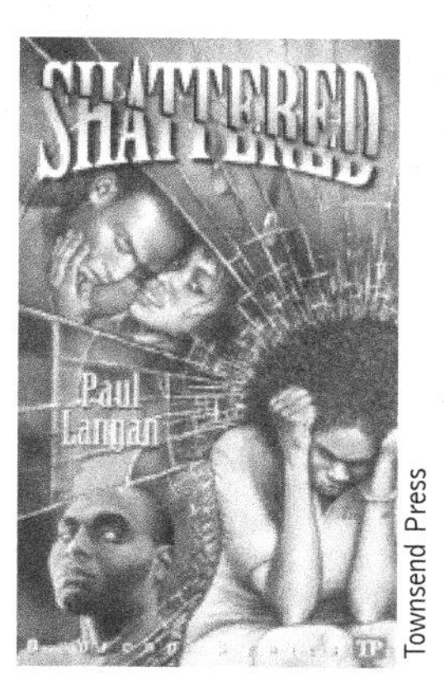

Shattered

"Girl, where you at?"

Darcy Wills winced at the voice blasting through her new cell phone. It was her best friend, Tarah Carson, and she sounded angry.

"C'mon, Darce. You're late," Tarah scolded.

Darcy knew Tarah was right even before she looked at her watch. She should have left the house ten minutes ago. Instead she was staring at her reflection in the bathroom mirror, hoping Hakeem Randall wouldn't notice the guilt in her eyes or the worry that haunted her face. So much had changed in the few months since they'd broken up. *Too much,* Darcy thought.

"I'm sorry, Tarah. It's just that—"

"Tell her I'm starvin'," yelled Cooper Hodden, Tarah's boyfriend, in the background. "Tell her if she don't get here soon, I'ma start eatin' without her."

His voice was so loud Darcy held the cell phone away from

Here's the first chapter from *Shattered,* by Paul Langan, a novel about teens facing difficult situations like the ones you read about in this book. *Shattered* is one of many books in the Bluford Series™ by Townsend Press.

her ear. It sounded like he and Tarah were in the hallway, not several blocks away at Niko's Pizza.

"Stop talkin' nonsense, Coop," Tarah replied. "We ain't eatin' nothin' till she gets here."

"C'mon, Tar! Why you gotsta be that way?" Cooper complained. "Don't ya hear my stomach growlin'?"

"Hold on one second, girl," Tarah said.

Darcy listened as Tarah started hollering at Cooper. She put the phone down to inspect her face again, paying special attention to a tiny pimple just above her right eyebrow.

Why does it have to be there now, she thought, dabbing it with a bit of cover-up. She'd already covered it once, but she wanted to make sure it was invisible to Hakeem.

It wasn't the only thing she hoped to hide.

"Hello? You still there?" Tarah asked.

Darcy quickly grabbed the phone off the bathroom counter.

"Yeah, I'm leavin' right now," she replied. A jolt of nervous energy raced down her back, making her stomach tremble. An hour of trying on different outfits, messing with her hair, and putting on makeup hadn't calmed her nerves. She still felt tense about seeing Hakeem again, especially after what happened over the summer.

"You mean you didn't even leave yet?" Tarah shouted. Darcy held the phone away from her ear again, but there was no escaping her friend's yelling. "We was supposed to meet fifteen minutes ago!"

"I know. I'm sorry, but things were busy at Scoops, and my manager made me stay late," Darcy lied, annoyed at herself for being dishonest with her best friend.

It was true the ice cream store had a busy day. Though it was early September, the weather was as hot as mid-July, and Scoops had been crammed with people buying ice cream. But Darcy's manager, Tamika Ardis, never asked her to stay late. Instead, she sent Darcy home early after she argued with a customer. Darcy had been rushing to prepare two milkshakes when she heard someone call out to her.

"Where's the rest of my change?"

Darcy turned to face a large woman with a tight weave. Two kids huddled close to the woman's legs, holding sticky, half-eaten ice cream cones that dripped onto the floor. Darcy had served them just a few minutes earlier.

"I already gave it to you, ma'am," Darcy replied.

"You better check your register or learn to count or somethin' 'cause I gave you a $20 bill. You just shortchanged me $10," the woman snapped, her free hand resting on her hips.

Darcy took a deep breath. All summer, she'd dealt with customers who treated her and her coworker Haley like trash. Usually Darcy just smiled and ignored it when people were mean, but today she didn't have any patience.

"You don't need to be rude, ma'am," Darcy replied. The words had slipped out so fast Darcy was stunned. So was Haley, who at that moment dropped a small chocolate sundae onto her cash register.

"Excuse me?" the woman said, nudging aside the person who'd been at the head of the line. "Girl, you best check that register and yo' mouth and give me my change, or I'ma make a scene up in here."

"Ma'am, let me finish with this customer first, and I'll help you," Darcy replied, still holding the milkshakes in her hands.

"No, you're gonna help me *now*. I waited in line once. I ain't waitin' again."

Darcy felt her temper building. She couldn't tell the customer off; that would only get her fired. And she couldn't admit she was too stressed to focus on her work. That would only make the woman angrier. For several long seconds, Darcy didn't know what to say. Her mind had gone blank.

"It's okay, ma'am. I can help you," Tamika cut in just in time. "Let's check the register."

Darcy watched as her manager unlocked the cash drawer. She was sure she hadn't miscounted. In her months on the job, she had made plenty of mistakes, but never with money. At Scoops and at Bluford High where she was about to start her junior year, numbers were always something Darcy was good at.

But inside the cash drawer, Tamika found a $20 bill sitting in the $10 slot. Darcy knew instantly she had made a mistake, and the customer had been right. Darcy felt her cheeks burn with embarrassment.

"I'm so sorry, ma'am," Darcy said as Tamika handed over the money.

"Mmm hmm." The woman scowled and walked out with her children.

"What's wrong with you, Darcy? I've never seen you act that way, and I never want to see it again," Tamika warned as soon as the store emptied out. "I can't afford to upset customers. It's hard enough to stay in business around here as it is."

"I'm sorry. I just got a lot on my mind."

"I hope it's not serious, Darcy. I need you around here. I wish I had two of you."

"No, it's not. It's just . . ." Darcy paused, trying to decide how honest she should be. Tamika recently offered to increase her hours. Darcy didn't want her to change her mind.

"It's her boyfriend, I mean *ex-boyfriend*," cut in Haley, her blond ponytail poking through the back of her green Scoops visor.

Darcy's jaw dropped. Haley had promised never to tell anyone what they discussed at work, especially not Tamika.

"He's been in Detroit for months, and tonight she's gonna see him for the first time since he got back. She doesn't want to admit it, but she's really excited," Haley continued with a smile. "And kinda nervous too."

"Haley, shut your mouth!" Darcy snapped, embarrassed to hear her personal life being discussed with her boss. "That was

between you and me."

"Relax, Darcy. I'm just telling her why you're so out of it. It's not like she hasn't noticed. You're on another planet today," Haley explained.

"I'm *not* out of it. I just miscounted some change, that's all. Not like you never made a mistake, Haley."

"Don't even go there, Darce. This isn't about me, and you know it."

Darcy knew Haley was right. All day, she kept forgetting customers' orders. It got so bad she started writing everything down like her first week on the job. Even when she tried to listen to people, all Darcy could hear were the questions racing through her mind.

Should I tell Hakeem about what happened to me this summer?

If I tell him the truth, will he blame me

or think I'm a bad person? Will we ever get back together?

"Haley's right," Tamika said, putting a hand on Darcy's shoulder.

"But—"

"It's okay, Darcy. I know you're a great worker, but today you're having a bad day. Lord knows I've had my share. When I think about it, almost all of them have to do with men," Tamika said with a knowing smile. "Why don't you take the rest of the afternoon off. Haley and I can handle things until closing."

"Are you serious?" Darcy asked. It felt wrong to have everyone know her business, but she needed the break to clear her head and get ready.

"Yeah, go and have fun. Not too much fun, though," Tamika said.

"And whatever you do, be sure someone else counts your change tonight," Haley teased.

Darcy left Scoops in a daze. It was true Hakeem distracted her from work, but there were other things tugging at her too. The summer had been like the earthquakes that sometimes cracked sidewalks and shattered windows in her neighborhood. Only this time, the quake centered on Darcy's house. She still felt aftershocks.

Grandma's quiet death in the bedroom next to Darcy's.

Her parents' announcement that they were having a baby.

Her old friend Brisana's pregnancy scare.

Deeper still was what happened one afternoon just after she and Hakeem broke up. That's when Brian Mason came around with his shiny red Toyota, his smooth voice and wide, dark shoulders. He was nineteen. Darcy babysat for his sister, Liselle. Just thinking of Brian made Darcy nauseous.

Should I tell Hakeem what happened?

For a while, it seemed like a question she wouldn't have to answer. The day Hakeem left, Darcy was sure she'd never see him again. His father was battling cancer, and his family was broke from medical bills. Their only choice was to move in with relatives in faraway Detroit. Hakeem and Darcy split up just before they left.

The loss crushed Darcy. Her boyfriend for most of their sophomore year, Hakeem had also been one of her closest friends at Bluford. He had stood by her no matter what drama was happening in her life, and there had been plenty, especially since her father returned after abandoning the family for five years. When they said goodbye for the last time, they promised to stay in touch and to always be honest with each other.

Darcy hadn't kept that promise.

For months, she ignored the voice in her head, the one that made her feel guilty whenever she stared at Hakeem's picture collecting dust in her room.

Then a miracle happened. Hakeem's father's health improved, and he allowed his son to live with Cooper and return to Bluford High. Darcy was thrilled beyond words at the news, but her past with Brian still haunted her.

There was no way she could tell Hakeem what happened. No

way she could admit she'd gone to Brian's apartment to be alone with him. No way she could say Brian soothed the ache she felt when Hakeem left. And there was something else she couldn't confess to Hakeem.

Brian had gone too far. They had been on his couch kissing, and everything was okay until he tried to work his hands under her shirt.

"Relax," he said when she grabbed his hand.

Then she felt him tugging at her clothes again. His scratchy palm slid against the sensitive skin of her stomach. This time, she told him point-blank to stop. She even tried to push him away. He got angry.

"You're acting like a baby!" he yelled. She tried to get off the couch, but he was too strong. Within seconds, he had her pinned. Sometimes she could still feel how he held her down, his hands gripping her like chains, his strong body pressing against hers. For a frightening instant, she realized she couldn't escape him.

But her father arrived and stopped Brian in his tracks.

"If you ever mess with my daughter again, it will be the last mistake you make!" Dad yelled with a wild rage in his eyes, slamming Brian against a wall. Brian moved out a few days later, but the damage was done.

For weeks afterward, Darcy relived the attacks in nightmares. In them, Brian was even more violent, and Dad never arrived to save her. The dreams got so severe she couldn't sleep. Then she started having panic attacks. Things got so bad Darcy told her parents and Tarah about her problem. She even met for weeks with a counselor at the community center where Tarah worked. Over time, the nightmares and panic attacks faded. But the scars were still there.

Darcy felt them gnawing at her as she left Scoops. Felt them as she prepared to meet Hakeem for the first time since he returned. Felt them even now as she spoke with Tarah on her cell phone.

"Look, Darce, are you comin' out or not?" Tarah asked, shattering her thoughts.

Darcy sighed and put her makeup away.

"I'll be there, Tar'," she said. "Ten minutes. I promise."

"If you're not, we're comin' over there and draggin' you out," Tarah warned.

"I'll be there," Darcy repeated, smoothing out her shirt one last time and inspecting the way her body filled her jeans. "I'm leaving right now."

Tarah hung up, and Darcy headed out the door, rushing toward Niko's.

Should I tell Hakeem what happened?

She still didn't know the answer.

Teens:
How to Get More Out of This Book

Self-help: The teens who wrote the stories in this book did so because they hope that telling their stories will help readers who are facing similar challenges. They want you to know that you are not alone, and that taking specific steps can help you manage or overcome very difficult situations. They've done their best to be clear about the actions that worked for them so you can see if they'll work for you.

Writing: You can also use the book to improve your writing skills. Each teen in this book wrote 5-10 drafts of his or her story before it was published. If you read the stories closely you'll see that the teens work to include a beginning, a middle, and an end, and good scenes, description, dialogue, and anecdotes (little stories). To improve your writing, take a look at how these writers construct their stories. Try some of their techniques in your own writing.

Reading: Finally, you'll notice that we include the first chapter from a Bluford Series novel in this book, alongside the true stories by teens. We hope you'll like it enough to continue reading. The more you read, the more you'll strengthen your reading skills. Teens at Youth Communication like the Bluford novels because they explore themes similar to those in their own stories. Your school may already have the Bluford books. If not, you can order them online for only $1.

Resources on the Web

We will occasionally post Think About It questions on our website, www.youthcomm.org, to accompany stories in this and other Youth Communication books. We try out the questions with teens and post the ones they like best. Many teens report that writing answers to those questions in a journal is very helpful.

How to Use This Book in Staff Training

Staff say that reading these stories gives them greater insight into what teens are thinking and feeling, and new strategies for working with them. You can help the staff you work with by using these stories as case studies.

Select one story to read in the group, and ask staff to identify and discuss the main issue facing the teen. There may be disagreement about this, based on the background and experience of staff. That is fine. One point of the exercise is that teens have complex lives and needs. Adults can probably be more effective if they don't focus too narrowly and can see several dimensions of their clients.

Ask staff: What issues or feelings does the story provoke in them? What kind of help do they think the teen wants? What interventions are likely to be most promising? Least effective? Why? How would you build trust with the teen writer? How have other adults failed the teen, and how might that affect his or her willingness to accept help? What other resources would be helpful to this teen, such as peer support, a mentor, counseling, family therapy, etc.

Resources on the Web

From time to time we will post Think About It questions on our website, www.youthcomm.org, to accompany stories in this and other Youth Communication books. We try out the questions with teens and post the ones that they find most effective. We'll also post lesson for some of the stories. Adults can use the questions and lessons in workshops.

Discussion Guide

Teachers and Staff:
How to Use This Book in Groups

When working with teens individually or in groups, using these stories can help young people face difficult issues in a way that feels safe to them. That's because talking about the issues in the stories usually feels safer to teens than talking about those same issues in their own lives. Addressing issues through the stories allows for some personal distance; they hit close to home, but not too close. Talking about them opens up a safe place for reflection. As teens gain confidence talking about the issues in the stories, they usually become more comfortable talking about those issues in their own lives.

Below are general questions that can help you lead discussions about the stories, which help teens and staff reflect on the issues in their own work and lives. In most cases you can read a story and conduct a discussion in one 45-minute session. Teens are usually happy to read the stories aloud, with each teen reading a paragraph or two. (Allow teens to pass if they don't want to read.) It takes 10-15 minutes to read a story straight through. However, it is often more effective to let workshop participants make comments and discuss the story as you go along. The workshop leader may even want to annotate her copy of the story beforehand with key questions.

If teens read the story ahead of time or silently, it's good to break the ice with a few questions that get everyone on the same page: Who is the main character? How old is she? What happened to her? How did she respond? Etc. Another good starting question is: "What stood out for you in the story?" Go around the room and let each person briefly mention one thing.

Then move on to open-ended questions, which encourage participants to think more deeply about what the writers were feeling, the choices they faced, and they actions they took. There are no right or wrong answers to the open-ended questions. Open-ended questions encourage participants to think about how the themes, emotions and choices in the stories relate to their own lives. Here are some examples of open-ended questions that we have found to be effective. You can use variations of these questions with almost any story in this book.

—What main problem or challenge did the writer face?

—What choices did the teen have in trying to deal with the problem?

—Which way of dealing with the problem was most effective for the teen? Why?

—What strengths, skills, or resources did the teen use to address the challenge?

—If you were in the writer's shoes, what would you have done?

—What could adults have done better to help this young person?

—What have you learned by reading this story that you didn't know before?

—What, if anything, will you do differently after reading this story?

—What surprised you in this story?

—Do you have a different view of this issue, or see a different way of dealing with it, after reading this story? Why or why not?

Credits

The stories in this book originally appeared in the following Youth Communication publications:

"A Dream Guy, a Nightmare Experience," by Anonymous, *New Youth Connections*, January/February 1991

"Telling Someone Helped Me Feel Better," by Anonymous, *New Youth Connections*, May/June 2000

"Why Are You Doing This, Mr. Jones?" by Anonymous, *FCYU*, July/August 1994

"Haunted," by Anonymous, *Represent*, July/August 2000

"Family Secrets," by Anonymous, *Represent*, March/April 2000

"My Love, My Friend, My Enemy," by Anonymous, *New Youth Connections*, September/October 1991

"I Said,`No!' ," by Anonymous, *New Youth Connections*, November, 1999

"Scare Tactics," by Anonymous, *New Youth Connections*, January/February 2000

"Bye-Bye, Baby," by Anonymous, *Represent*, November/December 2000

"Done Wrong," by Anonymous, *New Youth Connections*, November 1995

"Putting the Pieces Together Again," by Mimi Callaghan, *New Youth Connections*, April 1998

"Recovering from Rape: Helping the Wounds Heal," by Mimi Callaghan, *New Youth Connections*, April 1998

About Youth Communication

Youth Communication, founded in 1980, is a nonprofit youth development program located in New York City whose mission is to teach writing, journalism, and leadership skills. The teenagers we train become writers for our websites and books and for two print magazines, *New Youth Connections,* a general-interest youth magazine, and *Represent,* a magazine by and for young people in foster care.

Each year, up to 100 young people participate in Youth Communication's school-year and summer journalism workshops where they work under the direction of full-time professional editors. Most are African American, Latino, or Asian, and many are recent immigrants. The opportunity to reach their peers with accurate portrayals of their lives and important self-help information motivates the young writers to create powerful stories.

Our goal is to run a strong youth development program in which teens produce high quality stories that inform and inspire their peers. Doing so requires us to be sensitive to the complicated lives and emotions of the teen participants while also providing an intellectually rigorous experience. We achieve that goal in the writing/teaching/editing relationship, which is the core of our program.

Our teaching and editorial process begins with discussions

between adult editors and the teen staff. In those meetings, the teens and the editors work together to identify the most important issues in the teens' lives and to figure out how those issues can be turned into stories that will resonate with teen readers.

Once story topics are chosen, students begin the process of crafting their stories. For a personal story, that means revisiting events in one's past to understand their significance for the future. For a commentary, it means developing a logical and persuasive point of view. For a reported story, it means gathering information through research and interviews. Students look inward and outward as they try to make sense of their experiences and the world around them and find the points of intersection between personal and social concerns. That process can take a few weeks or a few months. Stories frequently go through ten or more drafts as students work under the guidance of their editors, the way any professional writer does.

Many of the students who walk through our doors have uneven skills, as a result of poor education, living under extremely stressful conditions, or coming from homes where English is a second language. Yet, to complete their stories, students must successfully perform a wide range of activities, including writing and rewriting, reading, discussion, reflection, research, interviewing, and typing. They must work as members of a team and they must accept individual responsibility. They learn to provide constructive criticism, and to accept it. They engage in explorations of truthfulness, fairness, and accuracy. They meet deadlines. They must develop the audacity to believe that they have something important to say and the humility to recognize that saying it well is not a process of instant gratification. Rather, it usually requires a long, hard struggle through many discussions and much rewriting.

It would be impossible to teach these skills and dispositions as separate, disconnected topics, like grammar, ethics, or assertiveness. However, we find that students make rapid progress when they are learning skills in the context of an inquiry that is personally significant to them and that will benefit their peers.

When teens publish their stories—in *New Youth Connections* and *Represent*, on the web, and in other publications—they reach tens of thousands of teen and adult readers. Teachers, counselors, social workers, and other adults circulate the stories to young people in their classes and out-of-school youth programs. Adults tell us that teens in their programs—including many who are ordinarily resistant to reading—clamor for the stories. Teen readers report that the stories give them information they can't get anywhere else, and inspire them to reflect on their lives and open lines of communication with adults.

Writers usually participate in our program for one semester, though some stay much longer. Years later, many of them report that working here was a turning point in their lives—that it helped them acquire the confidence and skills that they needed for success in college and careers. Scores of our graduates have overcome tremendous obstacles to become journalists, writers, and novelists. They include National Book Award finalist Edwidge Danticat, novelist Ernesto Quinonez, writer Veronica Chambers and *New York Times* reporter Rachel Swarns. Hundreds more are working in law, business, and other careers. Many are teachers, principals, and youth workers, and several have started nonprofit youth programs themselves and work as mentors—helping another generation of young people develop their skills and find their voices.

Youth Communication is a nonprofit educational corporation. Contributions are gratefully accepted and are tax deductible to the fullest extent of the law.

To make a contribution, or for information about our publications and programs, including our catalog of over 100 books and curricula for hard-to-reach teens, see www.youthcomm.org

About The Editors

Hope Vanderberg was the editor of *New Youth Connections*, Youth Communication's magazine by and for New York City teens, from 2004 to 2008.

Prior to working at Youth Communication, Vanderberg specialized in science journalism and environmental education. She was an editor at Medscape.com, a medical website, wrote articles for *Audubon* and *The Sciences* magazines, and taught children and teens at environmental education centers in California and Texas. She has also worked as a field biologist, studying bird behavior in Puerto Rico.

She has a master's degree in science and environmental journalism from New York University and a bachelor's degree from Earlham College. She is currently a freelance editor.

Keith Hefner co-founded Youth Communication in 1980 and has directed it ever since. He is the recipient of the Luther P. Jackson Education Award from the New York Association of Black Journalists and a MacArthur Fellowship. He was also a Revson Fellow at Columbia University.

Laura Longhine is the editorial director at Youth Communication. She edited *Represent*, Youth Communication's magazine by and for youth in foster care, for three years, and has written for a variety of publications. She has a BA in English from Tufts University and an MS in Journalism from Columbia University.

More Helpful Books
From Youth Comunication

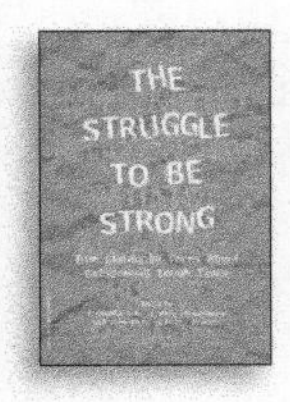

The Struggle to Be Strong: True Stories by Teens About Overcoming Tough Times. Foreword by Veronica Chambers. Help young people identify and build on their own strengths with 30 personal stories about resiliency. (Free Spirit)

Fighting the Monster: Teens Write About Confronting Emotional Challenges and Getting Help. Introduction by Dr. Francine Cournos. Teens write about their struggle to achieve emotional well-being. Topics include: Cutting, depression, bereavement, substance abuse, and more. (Youth Communication)

Depression, Anger, Sadness: Teens Write About Facing Difficult Emotions. Give teens the confidence they need to seek help when they need it. These teens write candidly about difficult emotional problems—such as depression, cutting, and domestic violence—and how they have tried to help themselves. (Youth Communication)

My Secret Addiction: Teens Write About Cutting. These true accounts of cutting, or self-mutilation, offer a window into the personal and family situations that lead to this secret habit, and show how teens can get the help they need. (Youth Communication)

Enjoy the Moment: Teens Write About Dealing With Stress. Help decrease the levels of stress and conflict in your teens' lives. These young writers describe how they cope with stress, using methods including meditation, journal writing, and exercise. (Youth Communication)

The Fury Inside: Teens Write About Anger. Help teens manage their anger. These writers tell how they got better control of their emotions and sought the support of others. (Youth Communication)

Analyze This: Teens Write About Therapy. Get insight into how therapy looks from a teen's perspective and help teens find the services they need. Teens in foster care write about their experiences with therapy. Some are happy with the help, while others are dissatisfied or confused. (Youth Communication)

Out of the Shadows: Teens Write About Surviving Sexual Abuse. Help teens feel less alone and more hopeful about overcoming the trauma of sexual abuse. This collection includes first-person accounts by male and female survivors grappling with fear, shame, and guilt. (Youth Communication)

Sticks and Stones: Teens Write About Bullying. Shed light on bullying, as told from the perspectives of the perpetrator, the victim, and the witness. These stories show why bullying occurs, the harm it causes, and how it might be prevented. (Youth Communication)

Out With It: Gay and Straight Teens Write About Homosexuality. Break stereotypes and provide support with this unflinching look at gay life from a teen's perspective. With a focus on urban youth, this book also includes several heterosexual teens' transformative experiences with gay peers. (Youth Communication)

To order these and other books, go to:
www.youthcomm.org
or call 212-279-0708 x115

CPSIA information can be obtained
at www.ICGtesting.com
Printed in the USA
LVHW081642130222
711043LV00015B/904